The BUDGET KIT

The Common Cent$ Money Management Workbook

Judy Lawrence

Judy Lawrence
P.O. Box 13167
Albuquerque, NM 87192
(505) 296-8792

Dearborn
Financial Publishing, Inc.

Dedication

To my parents who inspired my skills and interest in managing money through their everyday examples.

Publisher: Kathleen A. Welton
Associate Editor: Karen A. Christensen
Senior Project Editor: Jack L. Kiburz
Interior Design: Lucy Jenkins
Cover Design: Neographix

Published by Dearborn Financial Publishing, Inc.

Printed in the United States of America

95   10   9   8   7   6

Library of Congress Cataloging-in-Publication Data

Lawrence, Judy.
    The budget kit : the common cent$ money management workbook / by Judy Lawrence.
        p.   cm.
    Includes bibliographical references and index.
    ISBN 0-79310-495-5
    1. Finance, Personal. 2. Home economics. I. Title.
HG179.L338 1992
640′.42—dc20   92-36118
                                                    CIP

Foreword

I have known Judy Lawrence for nearly a dozen years. At a time when most people considered budgeting a topic that belonged in a home-economics course, Judy understood the importance of having control over your finances. Over the years, I have watched *The Budget Kit* evolve into the first and most useful financial tool that every family should have.

We all know how important it is to plan for a secure financial future. The down payment for a house cannot be scraped together from pocket change. College money will not magically appear when teenagers turn 18. Social Security never will be enough to ensure a comfortable retirement.

Everyday financial choices are magnified over the years. The decisions to spend wisely and save carefully in our daily lives ultimately will lead us to financial security. Willpower is not enough. You must have a plan—and you must follow it.

The first step in taking command of your finances is knowing where all the money is going now—and how to redirect it to your benefit. I know of no better way to get started than by making the personal commitment to use *The Budget Kit* on a regular basis.

I can promise that this book is easy to use, and I also can promise that you will feel so much better once you get started using it!

—Terry Savage, author of
Terry Savage Talks Money

Table of Contents

Monthly Expense Record

A record of money earned and spent each month. Necessary when establishing a personal budget and deciding which expenses must be reduced.

Summary-for-the-Year Record/End-of-the-Year Tax Information

A summary of each month's total income and expenses. Good for measuring your financial progress and making future plans.

Medical Expense Record

A record of mileage, dates, total bills and reimbursements from insurance for visits to the doctor, hospital, drugstore, etc. Necessary for tax and personal records.

Tax-Deductible Expense Record

Multiple Tax-Deductible Expenses Record

A convenient record of your various tax-deductible expenses whether donations, professional dues or taxes—all in one place for tax time.

Miscellaneous Expense Record

Place to keep additional records needed for taxes or personal use such as automobile, child-care and education expenses and casualty and theft losses.

Investment/Savings Record

A record of certificates of deposit (CDs), money-market accounts, stocks, bonds and other simple investments or savings.

Savings Activity Record

A record of your monthly savings for your emergency, reserve and goal funds. Also shows withdrawals and interest earned.

Retirement Savings Record

A record of your regular contributions to various retirement programs.

Net-Worth Statement

A picture of your total financial worth. A valuable aid for loan and insurance purposes.

Child-Support Records

A place to record necessary information related to child support such as check number, amount, date, arrival date, etc.

Child-Support Payment Record
Child-Support Enforcement Record

A record of all necessary information if you ever need help from the Child Support Enforcement Agency.

Child Visitation Record

Recommended Reading

Index

Notes

Acknowledgments

My special thanks goes to the following people who helped with the development of this new *Budget Kit: The Commoncent$ Money-Management Workbook* and those who gave their support and encouragement during the years it took to produce the workbook you now hold:

- Kathy Welton, my editor, for finding me once again and believing in possibilities;
- Terry Savage for her enthusiastic support as she talked and wrote about this workbook for so many years;
- Dwight and Carol Myers for always being there, having the answers and making good things happen;

- Janie Bluestein for giving her time, assistance and encouragement when they were needed the most;
- Bonnie, Elsa, Bea and Cynthia for sharing their personal stories with me and sensitizing me to the needs of the divorced parent;
- David Levin and Jan Gilman for sharing their legal expertise and guiding me through the legal maze of the needs of the divorced parent; and
- Especially Glen, Judith, Diane "Kiel Buddy," James, Paula, Kimberly, Colette, Debbie and the many other readers who have used this workbook year after year and have shared their ideas and suggestions that now are implemented in this new edition.

Preface

Dear Reader:

Hundreds of helpful money-management books and software are on the market. Many of these books encourage their readers to establish a budget. Some people, however, just don't know how to get started with this process and they tell me that they want a simple book to help them establish a budget and learn how to manage their everyday money.

As a counselor, I originally designed this workbook (calling it *Common Cent$*) for young families and women who were suddenly widowed or divorced and who did not have money-management skills and often were intimidated by the whole idea. I have since realized, through my workshops and from the many letters I have received from people of all professions and incomes, that managing finances is a universal concern.

Just having money does not necessarily ensure your ability to manage it. That's where this workbook comes in. It is written in easy-to-understand terms and is a complete, realistic and comprehensive approach to managing your finances.

It is extremely gratifying to hear from so many of you since *Common Cent$* originally was published and to learn how this workbook helped you buy your first home, finally get out of debt and start saving and investing money for the first time.

I've enjoyed the letters and telephone calls from many of you offering your suggestions and ideas for this newly revised edition, *The Budget Kit: The Common Cent$ Money-Management Workbook*. I know you will appreciate the new design, additions and revisions. Getting into the savings habit will be easier and more rewarding as you use the different savings records and watch your balances grow. Tax time will go more smoothly when you use the tax-deductions record.

If you are divorced and dealing with child-support payments, you will be especially pleased to see the section on child-support records in the back of the workbook.

I always welcome your suggestions and comments to help me continually improve this workbook to fit your needs and to help you reach your goals.

I wish you a successful and prosperous year.

Judy Lawrence

Introduction

During these trying economic times, there is a great need for organizing and managing your spending. Whether you earn $50,000 or $15,000 a year, you must plan ahead and know where your money is going. The purpose of this money-management workbook is to raise your awareness about how you handle your finances and to give you a tool for gaining control of your hard-earned money.

You finally will know where your money is going and then can decide as you evaluate your spending whether this is truly where you *want* your money to go.

Listed in the Table of Contents are the many different worksheets found in this workbook with an explanation of each. A variety of worksheets for different uses is provided. You can pick the worksheet that best fits your financial situation or use it as a guideline for planning your own method of managing your money. By filling in these worksheets, you will gain a better overall picture of your monthly and yearly spending at a glance.

How you use these worksheets depends on your own personal needs: how far in debt you may be or just how out of touch you are with your finances. As one woman put it, "It was only after the bill collectors were calling that I realized that I needed to use these worksheets and make them work for me. Since I started using the Monthly Budget Worksheet, I can plan and organize my spending so that the paycheck actually lasts until the next one arrives. The worksheets really work, but you have to make them work."

Once you take the time to start organizing and planning your financial affairs with these worksheets, the results will be extremely rewarding. Whether you need better control of your money to keep the bill collectors from your door or you want to plan a trip to Hawaii, using this workbook will bring you closer to your goal.

How To Use *The Budget Kit*

THE PURPOSE OF THIS WORKBOOK

The Budget Kit is easy to understand and practical to use. Because it is flexible, it can be used immediately regardless of the time of year or the condition of your finances. By following the guidelines in this workbook, you will learn to take charge of your finances, instead of suddenly having to react to a crisis situation.

There are two purposes for this workbook. The first is to help you get your finances organized and keep proper records. With this workbook, you can keep records of your monthly expenses, medical costs, installment payments, credit-card charges, mail-order purchases, child-support payments, savings, investments, retirement and net-worth information.

The second purpose is to help you plan and manage your finances. You can list and plan your goals; work out an estimating method for paying yourself, your bills and your monthly expenses; remind yourself of items you need or want to buy when money is available; and plan ahead for the sporadic, but anticipated, expenses throughout the year.

HOW TO GET STARTED

Set aside a block of time so you can thoroughly review the variety of sections available in this workbook. These sections contain instructions along with worksheets that were designed to address many different needs. Each worksheet can be used independently or with another. Determine your own needs and see how this book will best fit them.

After reviewing this workbook, set up your own system for the next 12 months. Begin with the more permanent, one-time-only recording and planning sections. These will be more involved, but once they are completed, you won't have to repeat the process. Then go on to the active planning and managing sections that will involve more daily and monthly participation.

To locate the different sections more quickly, use colored removable adhesive tabs that are carried by most stationery stores and label them for each section you use.

WHICH SECTIONS TO COMPLETE FIRST

To complete the one-time-only section, gather up your checkbook register, bills and all other related household expense papers. Go to the **Yearly Budget Worksheet** page and read the instructions. Using the categories as guidelines, determine your major anticipated yearly expenses and fill in the worksheet for the year with the amounts and the months due. The **Gift-Giving Worksheet** and the **Subscription Record** also could be filled in at this time. Both will come in handy as you complete the Yearly Budget Worksheet.

Next, turn to the **Debt Payment Record.** Go through your records and list those creditors you are paying in installments. If some of your loans are paid off during the year, you will have a visual picture of when they will be paid. It will be easier to see how you can apply that extra money to your other loans. Also, by having a full picture of your debt status, you will be less apt to over-extend your credit, thus maintaining a good credit record.

Complete the **Investment/Savings Record** if this section applies to your financial situation and you don't already have a financial portfolio. This section will require a great deal of detailed information, but it will be an invaluable record when it is completed.

The **Net-Worth Statement** page usually is another once-a-year project unless you are updating the information for personal or loan purposes. Now that you have gathered all your household papers, this is a good time to complete this worksheet.

The last area, but the most important, before going on to the day-to-day, money-management activities is **Setting Financial Goals.** Deciding on some of your goals at this time is very important. Be sure they are meaningful and important to you. Focusing on your goals will help you avoid discouragement or frustration and will motivate you to effectively manage your money.

MONTHLY INCOME AND EXPENSES

An important part of your monthly money-management activities is knowing or finding out exactly what your monthly income and expenses are. The **Monthly Expense Record** will help you find this out. You can either go back through your records and checkbook register, and by using the **Monthly Expense Record** as a guideline, reconstruct a month's worth of records. Or you can start keeping records for every month and get a better idea of what your income is as well as learn what your general monthly expenses are.

JUST MINUTES A DAY

Your most time-consuming task is finished. From here on, once you are in the habit of recording your expenses and other records (such as mail-order purchases or child-support payments) and jotting down your needs/wants and goals ideas in this book, the process soon will become routine and take only minutes a day.

If both spouses spend money, each should remember what was spent and take a few minutes to record expenses on the **Monthly Expense Record.** The wealth of information you gain from those records will be worth the time you invest.

A FEW HOURS A MONTH

Bill paying, whether it is done once or twice a month, requires time to gather up your bills, checkbook, envelopes, stamps, etc. The **Monthly Budget Worksheet,** however, streamlines the whole process and helps you anticipate all upcoming bills and expenses.

As you pay your bills and work out your monthly plan, refer to the following sections to help with your total planning: the **Yearly Budget Worksheet** for any occasional bills due that month; the **Monthly Expense Record** showing the previous months' totals so you have a better estimate of food, gas and other general expenses; the **Debt Payment Record** for any loan payments due (be sure to record your payment and the balance due on this chart); and the **Credit-Card Purchase Record** so you know how much of a bill to anticipate.

After an hour or two, you should have your bills paid and a clearer picture of where you stand for the current month as well as an idea of your status for the next month.

PREPARE FOR THE EXPECTED AND UNEXPECTED

By setting up your system for the year, you are planning ahead and getting a full financial picture. As you plan ahead for your monthly budget, it is important to remember to include three areas:

1. Reserve Account—After listing your predictable major anticipated yearly expenses on the **Yearly Budget Worksheet** such as car insurance, home-improvement plans, tuition, gifts, etc., total these up. Divide this number by 12 to get the monthly amount you need to set aside in a bank, credit union or money-market account for a reserve account (not emergency fund). This money will be for expenses you know will come up.

Enter this reserve account and amount on your **Monthly Budget Worksheet** under "Fixed Amounts" at the top of the page. When an annual insurance premium or tuition payment comes due, you will be prepared and have the amount in the bank. These infrequent expenses no longer will disrupt your whole budget.

2. Emergency Account—There also may be times when unknown disasters occur, for example, when the hot-water heater goes out or the car breaks down. Money must be set aside for the potential emergencies as well. Again, this account and whatever amount you put into the bank, credit union or money-market account for it should be entered on the **Monthly Budget Worksheet** under "Fixed Amounts" at the top of the page. This money is *not* to be confused with the reserve account, which actually is being held for expenses that have already occurred or will occur.

3. Goals Account—An entire section of this workbook is devoted to identifying goals and saving for them. Goals are very important. This is the third area that should be included on your **Monthly Budget Worksheet.**

By including your Reserve, Emergency and Goals Accounts in the **Monthly Budget Worksheet,** you have a way of putting together and seeing your total financial picture. This process also reminds and encourages you to save and put funds aside regularly, offering you a system for staying in control of your finances.

WHO MANAGES THE FAMILY BUDGET

In most households, one spouse assumes the role of "Family Budget Director" and keeps that role. This can, of course, be logical and efficient provided this person is good at managing money and enjoys doing so. Each spouse, however, should be involved with the household finances and responsibilities at some point even if he or she takes on the responsibility every other year.

By getting involved with the family finances on some regular basis (every six months or year take over the responsibility from your spouse), you develop an awareness and understanding of your financial obligations, expenses, limitations, family spending patterns and overall current financial status.

This awareness is important for personal relationships. If both spouses earn money, but occasionally the spouse managing the finances must announce that certain items or luxuries are not affordable, the news can cause all kinds of bad feelings, confusion and misunderstanding for the noninvolved spouse. "Why not? We were paid just three days ago. What are you doing with the money?" is not an uncommon response.

Without a total sense of the family finances, it is difficult to know what you really can and cannot afford.

This awareness is especially important if there is ever an extended incapacitating illness, a divorce or a death in the family. When the spouse not familiar with the family finances suddenly is responsible for them, this can be a very frightening experience.

TAKE CHARGE OF YOUR LIFE AND MONEY

The methods and guidelines in this workbook will show you how to set your goals, watch your spending and plan your expenses. You then will find that your bills are paid on time, more money is saved than you ever thought possible, your investments are off to a healthy start, your goals are being reached and the stress in your life is reduced.

As you take charge of your money, you will notice this control carrying over to other aspects of your life. Your relationships with your family will become more relaxed and more time will be available to pay attention to other things in life besides just money.

Best of luck as you begin your new money-management program!

Setting Financial Goals

Setting financial goals is one of the most important steps for gaining financial control. When you have a goal, you have the motivation needed to follow a money-management plan.

The worksheets on the following pages will help you identify and record your financial goals and develop a plan for reaching them.

To begin, ask yourself what is important to you. What will make you happy and/or be a significant accomplishment? Define your goals in specific attainable terms (such as buying a red, two-door BMW instead of just a new car) and write them down. You then have taken the first step toward reaching your goals.

IMMEDIATE/SHORT-RANGE GOALS

These goals are any that you have identified for the next month and/or year. Your goals depend on your interests and your life-style. Perhaps you want to save your Christmas money in advance this year, buy drapes or pay off a major debt.

Do not forget your emergency fund. If you do not have at least three months' take-home pay set aside as a protection against unforeseen problems or disasters, this should be your *number-one goal*. Once you have the security of knowing you are covered for possible emergencies, you can comfortably focus on your other goals.

When you reach the goals you have identified in this section, you will have more confidence and discipline for the more aggressive goals in the Middle-Range/Long-Range Goals section.

MIDDLE-RANGE/LONG-RANGE GOALS

Middle-range goals are those you hope to reach two to five years from now. Maybe you are dreaming of a new home, thinking of starting a family or planning a trip abroad.

Long-range goals include plans beyond five years, including retirement. By thinking about longer-range periods, you will make wiser use of your money. With time on your side, small amounts of money saved for 10 to 40 years will grow tremendously. And if you pay closer attention to where you invest your money, it will grow even more.

FAMILY AFFAIR

If you have a family, bring everyone together to discuss their interests and goals. Children need to take part in this activity not only to give their input, but to learn from the process for their own adult years.

There seldom is enough money to reach everyone's goals. When Dad wants a boat, Mom wants a piano and Junior wants a VCR, compromise is necessary. Each member of the family has to give and take and decide what is agreeable as a compromise. Rather than drop a major goal altogether, try delaying the deadline date.

FILLING IN YOUR IDENTIFIED GOALS WORKSHEET

Once you have defined your goals and have written them down under "Goals," fill in the remainder of the chart. Number the "Priority" of each goal listed. Which goal do you want first, second, etc.? Which can wait a few months or another year?

What is your "Date Needed"? Six months, one year, six years? Every goal should have a beginning and an ending date. Once you have committed yourself to a time frame in your mind and on paper, you have taken one more positive step toward reaching your goal.

"Cost Estimate" helps develop your estimating ability and forces you to do some research. By calling, reading or shopping to determine the estimated cost of buying a computer or putting in a pool, for example, your goal becomes more than just a dream.

If you have money in savings, how much of that "Amount Already Saved" do you want to use toward your goal? Write it down. Commit yourself to an amount.

"How To Achieve" is crucial. What are you willing to do to make your goal a reality? Will it involve working overtime or finding a second job? Will it mean trade-offs—cutting back or eliminating expenses such as movies, meals out or smoking—so you can reach your goal?

How much will you have to save each week, month or year to reach your goals? If you have a difficult time setting aside money for your goals, arrange with your bank for direct deposit from your paycheck.

The Goals Savings Record worksheet is a great place for keeping track of your savings for your goals. Take your "Cost Estimate" figure and write it in the space next to "Total Cost." Divide that figure by 12 to see how much money you need to save every month. Each month, record your savings and balance. You will be excited to actually see yourself coming closer to your goal each month.

PAY ATTENTION TO YOUR MONEY

If you have a strong desire to reach your goal and you *really* want your money to work for you, you must pay attention to what you do with your money.

Earlier, I mentioned having time on your side and paying closer attention to your money. For long-range goals (college, early retirement) where large amounts are necessary, these two factors are critical.

Let's say that you decide to save $100 at the beginning of every month for ten years to reach your goal. You could stash that money under your favorite mattress and have $12,000 at the end of ten years. Obviously, that method is not the wisest or safest.

If you had chosen to take that monthly $100 to your bank and let it sit safely in a savings account and draw 3 to 5 percent compounded daily interest, after ten years you would have made nearly $2,000 to $3,500 more "free" dollars for doing nothing more than driving to your local bank. In the meantime, you would have saved $15,536.81 for your goal.

On the other hand, if you were to take time to find an account that gives 10 percent compounded daily interest for that same $100 every month for ten years, your reward for your research time would be an extra $4,995.61 over the 5 percent interest or an extra $8,532.42 over the mattress investment, giving you $20,532.42 for your goal!

These figures do exclude the inflation factor; however, the more years you have to invest and the higher interest rate or return amount you get, the more money you will make. Read financial books and magazines or talk to your local banker, broker, insurance agent or financial planner to examine your options. *When you learn how to effectively invest your hard-earned money, you can be confident that you will reach your goals.*

Identified Goals Worksheet

Immediate/Short-Range Goals

Priority	Goals	Date Needed	Cost Estimate	Amount Already Saved	How To Achieve ($ per month, second job, etc.)

Middle-Range/Long-Range Goals

Priority	Goals	Date Needed	Cost Estimate	Amount Already Saved	How To Achieve ($ per month, second job, etc.)

Goals Savings Record

Goal: IRA   Total Cost: 2,000

	JAN.	FEB.	MAR.	APR.	MAY	JUNE	JULY	AUG.	SEPT.	OCT.	NOV.	DEC.	
Deposit	167	167	150	160	174	167	157	177	167	167	177	167	Monthly Deposit: 167
Balance	167	334	484	644	821	988	1,145	1,322	1,489	1,656	1,833	2,000	Total: 2,000

Goal: Total Cost:

	JAN.	FEB.	MAR.	APR.	MAY	JUNE	JULY	AUG.	SEPT.	OCT.	NOV.	DEC.	
Deposit													Monthly Deposit:
Balance													Total:

Goal: Total Cost:

	JAN.	FEB.	MAR.	APR.	MAY	JUNE	JULY	AUG.	SEPT.	OCT.	NOV.	DEC.	
Deposit													Monthly Deposit:
Balance													Total:

Goal: Total Cost:

	JAN.	FEB.	MAR.	APR.	MAY	JUNE	JULY	AUG.	SEPT.	OCT.	NOV.	DEC.	
Deposit													Monthly Deposit:
Balance													Total:

Goal: Total Cost:

	JAN.	FEB.	MAR.	APR.	MAY	JUNE	JULY	AUG.	SEPT.	OCT.	NOV.	DEC.	
Deposit													Monthly Deposit:
Balance													Total:

Goal: Total Cost:

	JAN.	FEB.	MAR.	APR.	MAY	JUNE	JULY	AUG.	SEPT.	OCT.	NOV.	DEC.	
Deposit													Monthly Deposit:
Balance													Total:

Goal: Total Cost:

	JAN.	FEB.	MAR.	APR.	MAY	JUNE	JULY	AUG.	SEPT.	OCT.	NOV.	DEC.	
Deposit													Monthly Deposit:
Balance													Total:

Goal: Total Cost:

	JAN.	FEB.	MAR.	APR.	MAY	JUNE	JULY	AUG.	SEPT.	OCT.	NOV.	DEC.	
Deposit													Monthly Deposit:
Balance													Total:

Goal: Total Cost:

	JAN.	FEB.	MAR.	APR.	MAY	JUNE	JULY	AUG.	SEPT.	OCT.	NOV.	DEC.	
Deposit													Monthly Deposit:
Balance													Total:

The formula for determining the monthly amount to save for each of your goals is:
Total cost of your goal ÷ Number of months left to date needed = Amount per month need to save.

Monthly Budget Worksheet

WHY A MONTHLY BUDGET WORKSHEET?

The Monthly Budget Worksheet is designed to provide a guideline for coordinating your monthly bills and expenses with your take-home pay. Your monthly bills always are easier to remember because many bills often come in the mail. Forgotten, however, are the expenses each month such as meals eaten out, haircuts, gifts, books, tapes, seminars, etc., which often throw off the monthly budget.

This worksheet is especially helpful during those lean times when work hours are reduced and the amount of bills to pay exceeds the money coming in. This guideline will give you a better overall picture of your monthly obligations and life-style expenses. The categories are kept general to allow for flexibility and necessary additions based on your own personal financial needs.

WHAT TO DO WITH THAT STACK OF BILLS

To use the Monthly Budget Worksheet, write the net amounts of each paycheck in the blanks at the ① top on the "Net Income Total Amount" line. You will notice the emphasis on net income and not on gross income throughout this workbook. This way, you are dealing only with the cash you actually have for paying your bills. (See the Monthly Expense Record for information regarding payroll deductions and taxes.) How many columns under "Income Source" you fill in depends on how often you are paid each

month. Of course, there are many job situations where the amount may vary or is not always known, such as with sales commissions. If this is the case, make a very conservative estimate until the actual amount is known.

Under the "Income Source" amount, there is ② room to add the date each paycheck is received. This will help with your planning when working with due dates on the bills.

Next, divide the bills into two stacks: one for those that must be paid that month and another for those bills that can be postponed if necessary. Look at the amounts of the "must" bills and write their amounts in the appropriate blanks under the "Income Source" according to the due dates or other deadlines. At this point, you may want or need to make arrangements ahead of time with the respective companies for partial or late payments for those bills you are unable to pay on time.

Try to distribute and balance the more expensive bills over the different pay periods rather than pay them all with one check. If you have enough money to handle more than the "must" bills, now is the time to distribute the amount of the "postponable" bills under the "Income Source."

PAY YOURSELF FIRST

Notice that "Allowance/Mad Money" and "Sav- ③ ings" are under "Fixed Amounts." The phrase "Pay yourself first" has been said many times, but it is a valid statement and a very important rule because if you penny-pinch to the point where there is no money left for "Allowance/Mad Money," you will end up bickering, frustrated and disappointed with the whole budget idea. The "Allowance/Mad Money" should be yours to do with as you please. You must decide how much "Allowance/Mad Money" each member needs to allow for little splurges and yet not ignore the necessary expenses.

Just as important under "Fixed Amounts" is "Savings." Again, this is paying yourself first. Consider "Savings" as an *expense,* setting aside a specific amount or percentage of your check at the same time you are completing the other categories of the worksheet. In this manner, you will be thinking of "Savings" as an expense so that it is planned for regularly and not dependent on leftover funds.

Remember the different savings accounts: **reserve** (for upcoming known bills and expenses listed on the Yearly Budget Worksheet), **emergency** (equivalent to three months of take-home pay for unknown disasters) and **goals** (wish list) and try to save regularly for them. Once you have saved enough money for the reserve and emergency accounts, you will realize that it is actually possible to save money. Saving for your goals soon becomes more exciting and challenging as you realize that reaching your goals now is possible.

NOW FOR SOME PRACTICE AT BUDGETING

In many cases, such as utilities or other areas under "Fixed Variable" and "Occasional," the exact amount of the bill is unknown. For those categories, ④ a space for "Budget" has been included. This is where your budgeting practice comes in. This space can be used to help plan for the bills until the exact amount is known. Remember to keep in mind those other expenses that are not seen as bills but show up on a daily basis: food, gas, entertainment, clothing, etc. Those must be planned for as well. Here you will take an estimated guess (budget) as to what you will need and the amount you can spend. Once you become familiar with estimating your expenditures, you will start learning to live within your budget. If your budget is realistic, you soon will learn to do

without certain unnecessary items to remain within the projected budget.

THE TIME FOR REEVALUATION

Finally, complete the "Totals" at the bottom of ⑤ the page. After determining all the totals, you may have some columns that have more total bills than income and some columns that have more income than bills. Try to shuffle the bills to be paid to different columns so there will be a balance.

During some periods, no matter how much you shuffle the bills or postpone the bills to the last possible day, it still is impossible to pay them with only your paycheck. This is the time for some real evaluation. You must decide what you need to change or do without to live within your income. Go over the budgeted expenses such as personal, clothing, etc., to see if any of these costs can be postponed, cut back or eliminated. Contact the companies to make special payment arrangements. Many companies (utilities, medical clinics, department stores, etc.) are very willing to accommodate you if you will notify them and make partial payments.

In the meantime, possibly you have been building a small emergency fund and can cover expenses this time by withdrawing the necessary amount. This should be an absolute last resort, however, with cutbacks planned for the next few months so that you can replenish your emergency fund again.

GETTING CONTROL OF YOUR FINANCES

You have just completed an important step in getting and keeping control of your finances. Of course, doing a Monthly Budget Worksheet does not change or increase the amount of actual money earned. Being aware, however, of where and how the money is spent will give you the feeling that you are beginning to control your money and will help you stretch the use of those dollars more than before.

Happy Budgeting!

Income Source:		Income	Income	Income	Income	Reserve Savings
① Net Income Total Amount:		896	1,107	880	1,107	1,188
Expenses	④Budget	Date: 9/4 ②	9/7	9/18	9/21	9/15
Mortgage/Rent	784	784				
Car Payments	211		211			
Other Loans *student*	50		50			
Insurance *Auto*	263*					263
Auto	395*					395
Club/Dues *Home Assoc.*	75*					75
Emerg. Goals	215 / 75		100		115 / 75	
Savings *Reserve*	1,000		400	300	300	
③ Allowance/Mad Money	50	20		30		
Electricity	90			90		
Fuel/Gas	75			75		
Water/Garbage	125*					125
Telephone	65			65		
Cable TV	35			35		
Food	350	50	100	50	150	
Auto Expense/Gas	85		30	30	25	
Auto License	100*					100
meals out	125		30	50	45	
child allowance *activities*	30 / 40	10	10	10	40	
Church/Charity	275		100		175	
Household *Photos*	20				20	
Personal *Perm*	80*					80
Clothes	75	25		30	20	
Medical *Prescrip.*	35				35	
Child Care *School Exp.*	75*					75
Recreation *Season Ticket*	75*					75
Counseling	130		65		65	
Books, CDs	35	10		25		
Credit Cards						
Visa	100			100		
Total Expense *Excludes**	3,950	899	1,096	890	1,065	1,188
⑤ Total Income	3,990					
Total Excess	40		11		42	
Total Short		-3		-10		

*From Reserve Savings (Yearly Budget Worksheet)

Income Source:						
Net Income Total Amount:						

	Expenses	**Budget**	**Date:**				
Fixed Amounts	Mortgage/Rent						
	Car Payments						
	Other Loans						
	Insurance						
	Club/Dues						
	Savings						
	Allowance/Mad Money						
Fixed Variable	Electricity						
	Fuel/Gas						
	Water/Garbage						
	Telephone						
	Cable TV						
	Food						
	Auto Expense/Gas						
	Church/Charity						
Occasional	Household						
	Personal						
	Clothes						
	Medical						
	Child Care						
	Recreation						
Installment	Credit Cards						
	Total Expense						
	Total Income						
	Total Excess						
	Total Short						

Income Source:						
Net Income Total Amount:						

	Expenses	Budget	Date:				
Fixed Amounts	Mortgage/Rent						
	Car Payments						
	Other Loans						
	Insurance						
	Club/Dues						
	Savings						
	Allowance/Mad Money						
Fixed Variable	Electricity						
	Fuel/Gas						
	Water/Garbage						
	Telephone						
	Cable TV						
	Food						
	Auto Expense/Gas						
	Church/Charity						
Occasional	Household						
	Personal						
	Clothes						
	Medical						
	Child Care						
	Recreation						
Installment	Credit Cards						
	Total Expense						
	Total Income						
	Total Excess						
	Total Short						

Income Source:						
Net Income Total Amount:						
	Expenses	Budget	Date:			
Fixed Amounts	Mortgage/Rent					
	Car Payments					
	Other Loans					
	Insurance					
	Club/Dues					
	Savings					
	Allowance/Mad Money					
Fixed Variable	Electricity					
	Fuel/Gas					
	Water/Garbage					
	Telephone					
	Cable TV					
	Food					
	Auto Expense/Gas					
	Church/Charity					
Occasional	Household					
	Personal					
	Clothes					
	Medical					
	Child Care					
	Recreation					
Installment	Credit Cards					
	Total Expense					
	Total Income					
	Total Excess					
	Total Short					

Income Source:						
Net Income Total Amount:						

	Expenses	**Budget**	**Date:**				
Fixed Amounts	Mortgage/Rent						
	Car Payments						
	Other Loans						
	Insurance						
	Club/Dues						
	Savings						
	Allowance/Mad Money						
Fixed Variable	Electricity						
	Fuel/Gas						
	Water/Garbage						
	Telephone						
	Cable TV						
	Food						
	Auto Expense/Gas						
	Church/Charity						
Occasional	Household						
	Personal						
	Clothes						
	Medical						
	Child Care						
	Recreation						
Installment	Credit Cards						
	Total Expense						
	Total Income						
	Total Excess						
	Total Short						

Income Source:						
Net Income Total Amount:						

	Expenses	**Budget**	**Date:**				
Fixed Amounts	Mortgage/Rent						
	Car Payments						
	Other Loans						
	Insurance						
	Club/Dues						
	Savings						
	Allowance/Mad Money						
Fixed Variable	Electricity						
	Fuel/Gas						
	Water/Garbage						
	Telephone						
	Cable TV						
	Food						
	Auto Expense/Gas						
	Church/Charity						
Occasional	Household						
	Personal						
	Clothes						
	Medical						
	Child Care						
	Recreation						
Installment	Credit Cards						
	Total Expense						
	Total Income						
	Total Excess						
	Total Short						

Income Source:						
Net Income Total Amount:						

	Expenses	**Budget**	**Date:**				
Fixed Amounts	Mortgage/Rent						
	Car Payments						
	Other Loans						
	Insurance						
	Club/Dues						
	Savings						
	Allowance/Mad Money						
Fixed Variable	Electricity						
	Fuel/Gas						
	Water/Garbage						
	Telephone						
	Cable TV						
	Food						
	Auto Expense/Gas						
	Church/Charity						
Occasional	Household						
	Personal						
	Clothes						
	Medical						
	Child Care						
	Recreation						
Installment	Credit Cards						
	Total Expense						
	Total Income						
	Total Excess						
	Total Short						

Income Source:						
Net Income Total Amount:						

	Expenses	Budget	Date:				
Fixed Amounts	Mortgage/Rent						
	Car Payments						
	Other Loans						
	Insurance						
	Club/Dues						
	Savings						
	Allowance/Mad Money						
Fixed Variable	Electricity						
	Fuel/Gas						
	Water/Garbage						
	Telephone						
	Cable TV						
	Food						
	Auto Expense/Gas						
	Church/Charity						
Occasional	Household						
	Personal						
	Clothes						
	Medical						
	Child Care						
	Recreation						
Installment	Credit Cards						
	Total Expense						
	Total Income						
	Total Excess						
	Total Short						

Income Source:						
Net Income Total Amount:						

	Expenses	Budget	Date:				
Fixed Amounts	Mortgage/Rent						
	Car Payments						
	Other Loans						
	Insurance						
	Club/Dues						
	Savings						
	Allowance/Mad Money						
Fixed Variable	Electricity						
	Fuel/Gas						
	Water/Garbage						
	Telephone						
	Cable TV						
	Food						
	Auto Expense/Gas						
	Church/Charity						
Occasional	Household						
	Personal						
	Clothes						
	Medical						
	Child Care						
	Recreation						
Installment	Credit Cards						
	Total Expense						
	Total Income						
	Total Excess						
	Total Short						

Income Source:						
Net Income Total Amount:						

	Expenses	**Budget**	**Date:**				
Fixed Amounts	Mortgage/Rent						
	Car Payments						
	Other Loans						
	Insurance						
	Club/Dues						
	Savings						
	Allowance/Mad Money						
Fixed Variable	Electricity						
	Fuel/Gas						
	Water/Garbage						
	Telephone						
	Cable TV						
	Food						
	Auto Expense/Gas						
	Church/Charity						
Occasional	Household						
	Personal						
	Clothes						
	Medical						
	Child Care						
	Recreation						
Installment	Credit Cards						
	Total Expense						
	Total Income						
	Total Excess						
	Total Short						

Income Source:						
Net Income Total Amount:						

	Expenses	**Budget**	**Date:**				
Fixed Amounts	Mortgage/Rent						
	Car Payments						
	Other Loans						
	Insurance						
	Club/Dues						
	Savings						
	Allowance/Mad Money						
Fixed Variable	Electricity						
	Fuel/Gas						
	Water/Garbage						
	Telephone						
	Cable TV						
	Food						
	Auto Expense/Gas						
	Church/Charity						
Occasional	Household						
	Personal						
	Clothes						
	Medical						
	Child Care						
	Recreation						
Installment	Credit Cards						
	Total Expense						
	Total Income						
	Total Excess						
	Total Short						

Monthly Budget Worksheet

Income Source:						
Net Income Total Amount:						

	Expenses	Budget	Date:				
Fixed Amounts	Mortgage/Rent						
	Car Payments						
	Other Loans						
	Insurance						
	Club/Dues						
	Savings						
	Allowance/Mad Money						
Fixed Variable	Electricity						
	Fuel/Gas						
	Water/Garbage						
	Telephone						
	Cable TV						
	Food						
	Auto Expense/Gas						
	Church/Charity						
Occasional	Household						
	Personal						
	Clothes						
	Medical						
	Child Care						
	Recreation						
Installment	Credit Cards						
	Total Expense						
	Total Income						
	Total Excess						
	Total Short						

Income Source:						
Net Income Total Amount:						

	Expenses	Budget	Date:				
Fixed Amounts	Mortgage/Rent						
	Car Payments						
	Other Loans						
	Insurance						
	Club/Dues						
	Savings						
	Allowance/Mad Money						
Fixed Variable	Electricity						
	Fuel/Gas						
	Water/Garbage						
	Telephone						
	Cable TV						
	Food						
	Auto Expense/Gas						
	Church/Charity						
Occasional	Household						
	Personal						
	Clothes						
	Medical						
	Child Care						
	Recreation						
Installment	Credit Cards						
	Total Expense						
	Total Income						
	Total Excess						
	Total Short						

Needs/Wants List

TAKING FURTHER CONTROL OF FINANCES

As you work with the Monthly Budget Worksheet, you are making decisions about how you need and want to spend your monthly income. These decisions are an important step in getting and maintaining control of your finances and learning to live within your means.

This Needs/Wants List is like a "wish list" that helps you take that control one step further. This section is designed to be a guideline for those times when you have extra money but want to be sure that you wisely use your money on priority items versus impulse items.

NEEDS AND WANTS VERSUS GOALS

Needs, wants and goals as used in this book are all the things that you would like to have but must wait until you can afford them. With your improved budgeting skills and money awareness, you know you will have the capability to eventually acquire these items.

The difference between needs/wants and goals is primarily in the cost and the significance of the desired items. Goals, as presented in the earlier part of this book, are more significant plans involving time and the gradual accumulation of funds for major purchases such as a stereo, car or home. Elimination of a major debt is also a goal.

Needs and wants, on the other hand, are the smaller-ticket items. These are the purchases made when extra money (known as discretionary money) is

left over after paying the bills and putting money aside for your savings and your goals.

HOW TO USE THIS LIST

Throughout the year, you probably see or think about many things you need or would like to have, but don't have the extra cash at the time to buy them. Jot down all your ideas on this Needs/Wants List.

Items on your list can range from things seen in mail-order catalogs, TV advertisements or stores to activities such as the opera, a concert or a ski weekend. Having these ideas written down also will make it easier for you to remember to watch for sales and list gift ideas as they come up.

At the same time, make a check mark either under the "Need" (necessities for your everyday wellbeing such as food, rent or medicine) or "Want" (which are nice to have, such as tapes, jewelry or theater tickets, but which you can do without if you have to) column. This way, you can make sure you take care of needs first when extra money is available. Record the source and cost of your items. When you are ready to purchase the listed item, the necessary information will be handy.

By using this Needs/Wants List, you start establishing priorities and identifying what you really do want when you have extra money. When you have an extra $50 (which you determine after completing your Monthly Budget Worksheet) and a sale suddenly catches your eye, you won't be so apt to impulsively buy something. It will be easier to remember that there was something else you really wanted or needed when extra money is available.

A FAMILY AFFAIR

The ability to prioritize is a valuable skill for all age levels. If your children ask for something when money is tight, write down their wishes on the list or have the children write them down. Your action assures your children that you are acknowledging their needs and wants rather than saying that they just can't have something. In this way, children also learn to establish priorities, make choices and develop patience. When money does become available, either from your budget or from their gifts or other money sources, your children can choose which item on the list to buy based on cost and priority instead of reacting impulsively to the first temptation that catches their eye in the store.

Needs/Wants List

Parents

Date	Item	Need	Want	Source (store, catalog, other)	Cost

Children

Date	Item	Need	Want	Source (store, catalog, other)	Cost

Yearly Budget Worksheet
(Nonmonthly Major Anticipated Expenses)

WHY A YEARLY BUDGET WORKSHEET?

The Yearly Budget Worksheet also is provided as a guideline to be used alone or with any or all the other worksheets in this workbook. Your personal finances and your method of handling them will determine which worksheets to use and how to adapt them to your own household expenses.

While the Monthly Budget Worksheet gives you a detailed picture of your monthly obligations, the Yearly Budget Worksheet is designed to give you a general picture of your major yearly obligations at a glance and can give you a more manageable picture than the use of files or notes on the calendar.

This is one more optional method to use for gaining control of your finances. It can prevent those periods when you may have had every bill figured just to the penny only to be deluged by the next day's mail with insurance or other bills you had overlooked or not anticipated.

When you have parts of the worksheet filled in (see sample) with all of your known anticipated major expenses, you will see which months have fewer expenses than others. When you see that some months have quite a few expenses coming up, you can plan to save a set amount ahead of time for those months or try to arrange to change the due date to another month that has fewer expenses. For example, if your car insurance is due in March and September and both months already have life insurance premiums and/or some other expenses due, contact the company and arrange to change the due months to May and November or whichever months have fewer expenses.

You will notice that several lines are left blank in all categories. This allows room for you to add and change as many categories as necessary to fit your own financial situation.

FILLING IN YOUR YEARLY WORKSHEET

Fixed Known—Now the work and planning begins. This is the section where you will include those expenses you know are due and know their exact amounts. To determine your "Fixed Known" expenses such as insurance premiums, go through your policies, checkbook or other records and find which months the premiums and other expenses are due. Premiums may be paid annually, semiannually or monthly. If your policies are paid monthly, it may be more economical and convenient to change them to annual premiums. While doing this or when buying a new policy, look for the months that have the fewest expenses and arrange to change the due date to one of those months. While checking the policy amounts to enter on the chart, also jot down the policy number in the space provided. This will save you valuable time and effort in the future when you need to refer to those policies. ①

Fixed Estimated—In this section, you will include ② all expenses you know will be due but do not know the exact amount. Including the utilities in this section may be more useful for some households than others. Some people arrange to pay averaged utility bills and others have fuel tanks filled at peak times so each situation will be different. For all cases, this section is helpful for record keeping. When planning for the next year, the previous year's chart will show which months were high in utility costs so you can budget accordingly.

The extra lines allow you to fill in your own fixed estimated expenses such as dues, school expenses, major hobbies, donations, etc. If you subscribe to many publications, use the Subscription Record as a handy planner.

③   **Estimated**—This section will be especially helpful if you are on a very tight budget. Included here could be all those expenses that are not immediate and not essential but are preferred when the extra time and money are available.

Gifts for some households are minimal expenses; for others who place a high priority on gifts, gifts can be a major expense when remembering Christmas, birthdays, weddings, Mother's and Father's Days, anniversaries, baby showers, etc. If gifts are important in your household, use the Gift-Giving Worksheet to help you plan this section.

Vacations also can be planned in advance. Keep in mind the miniweekend trip as well as those holiday and summer vacations. Fill in the amount you estimate it will cost and use that as a guideline. Both gifts and vacations are good items with which to learn to live within your income. You may enjoy buying expensive gifts or going on exotic vacations, but if this puts a hardship on your budget, you may have to reevaluate your priorities. Either spend less on these categories or less on some other categories.

Major Medical and Major Automobile expenses are some of those estimated expenses that are not only preferred but essential. You may not be able to wait and plan for that necessary major tune-up or set of tires under "Major Automobile Expenses" or for those necessary eyeglasses or dental work under "Major Medical Expenses." When these expenses come up, you will have to rearrange or postpone some other planned expenses on the chart. If circumstances allow you to plan these expenses, however, this chart will help in scheduling them.

Home Improvement expenses can range from a new mattress to an addition to the house. If you have been thinking about expenses like new furniture or remodeling a room and have been trying to decide when you can afford them, use this Yearly Budget Worksheet for your planning.

Holiday Events vary from household to household depending on how you celebrate Christmas, Easter, Valentine's Day, Halloween and other traditional and religious events in your family. Don't forget the cost of buying a Christmas tree, decorating the house or purchasing a new Halloween costume, along with all the other related expenses. By listing these estimates as well as the others on this page, you will have a more realistic approach to all your upcoming expenses.

Children's Activities may not apply to all households, but if it does for yours, this could include camp, seasonal clothing, Little League and other sports (uniforms and fees), hobbies, yearbooks, graduations, etc.

Other categories that you could include on this worksheet are: pets, donations, personal care (permanents, haircuts, cosmetics, etc.), season tickets, health spas, other membership dues, workshops and seminars and any other expenses in your household.

HOW TO USE THIS INFORMATION

Once you have estimated and projected your upcoming nonmonthly expenses, you already have valuable information that graphically shows you which months will be light and which ones will be difficult to deal with. At this point, you can evaluate each expense and decide if you want to change or eliminate it. You also can use this worksheet as a guideline to let you know which month would be better when taking on additional expenses.

When you total up all of these expenses, you can quickly see how this amount impacts on your total yearly spending and why your monthly budget often goes into a tailspin when some of these big expenses come due.

The Reserve Savings Account mentioned earlier in the discussion on savings now makes more sense. When you total each section separately ("Fixed Known," "Fixed Estimated," "Estimated") and divide by 12 using the form on the bottom of the page, you can see how much money must be put aside each month to prepare for these upcoming expenses. You then can transfer the total amount information for all three sections to the "Savings" section on the Monthly Budget Worksheet to help you plan ahead for the month.

REMINDER

This worksheet is only a guideline and is meant to be as flexible as possible. You are the one who decides how to use it to your best advantage.

Fixed Known Expenses ①

	JAN.	FEB.	MAR.	APR.	MAY	JUNE	JULY	AUG.	SEPT.	OCT.	NOV.	DEC.	TOTAL
Insurance													
Life – L.M.		80			80			80			80		320
Life – USAA	54			54			54			54			216
Auto – GMC			263						263				526
Auto – Honda			395						395				790
Retirement													
Prof. Licenses		95						130					225

Fixed Estimated Expenses ②

	JAN.	FEB.	MAR.	APR.	MAY	JUNE	JULY	AUG.	SEPT.	OCT.	NOV.	DEC.	TOTAL
Taxes/ Preparation				1,000 300									1,300
Utilities *Sewer*			65			20			125			85	295
Dues/ Subscriptions		dues 125			KPFM 18	Jrl. 40		dues 100		39 BL			322
Education/ Tuition	350							350					700
Donations	15				NC 25		WWF 25			40		100	205
Home Assoc.			75			75			75			75	300

Estimated Expenses ③

	JAN.	FEB.	MAR.	APR.	MAY	JUNE	JULY	AUG.	SEPT.	OCT.	NOV.	DEC.	TOTAL
Gifts	BD 25	BD 15	(2)BD 50	M.Day(2) Grad.	60 50	F.Day 30	Shower 35	Wedding 50		Anniv. 40		650	1,005
Vacations			Ski 250			700							950
Major Medical Expenses		Dental 750			Vision 250								1,000
Major Auto Expenses	Tune-Up 100		Tires 200	Lube 25	AAA 35		Lube 25	Lic 80	Lic 100	Lube 25			590
Home Improvement			Door 250	Yard 150			Drapes 250						650
Holiday Events				Easter 25						Halloween 60	TG 75	150	310
Children's Activities	65				50	Camp 150	50		75				390
Clothing	shoes/coat 320				350			700					1,370
Personal	Perm 80		25		80		25		80		25		315
Pet Expenses					shots 35	Kennel 75						Groom 35	145
Season Tickets									75				75
Total	1,009	1,065	1,573	1,579	973	1,125	464	1,490	1,188	258	180	1,095	11,999

÷ 12 = 999.91

Reserve Savings: Fixed Known Total $ 2,077 ÷ 12 = $ 173.08 /month Fixed Estimated Total $ 3,122 ÷ 12 = $ 260.17 /month Estimated Total $ 6,800 ÷ 12 = $ 566.66 /month

Fixed Known Expenses

	JAN.	FEB.	MAR.	APR.	MAY	JUNE	JULY	AUG.	SEPT.	OCT.	NOV.	DEC.	TOTAL
Insurance													
Retirement													

Fixed Estimated Expenses

	JAN.	FEB.	MAR.	APR.	MAY	JUNE	JULY	AUG.	SEPT.	OCT.	NOV.	DEC.	TOTAL
Taxes/ Preparation													
Utilities													
Dues/ Subscriptions													
Education/ Tuition													

Estimated Expenses

	JAN.	FEB.	MAR.	APR.	MAY	JUNE	JULY	AUG.	SEPT.	OCT.	NOV.	DEC.	TOTAL
Gifts													
Vacations													
Major Medical Expenses													
Major Auto Expenses													
Home/Yard Maintenance													
Holiday Events													
Children's Activities													
Total													

Reserve Savings: **Fixed Known** Total $_____ ÷ 12 = $_____/month **Fixed Estimated** Total $_____ ÷ 12 = $_____/month **Estimated** Total $_____ ÷ 12 = $_____/month

Gift-Giving Worksheet

Gift giving is often one of the most underestimated and overlooked budget categories in many households. People often are amazed, once they start recording all their expenses, just how much money actually is spent on gifts. It is not uncommon to forget occasional events or extended family members on the gift list when trying to estimate the overall gift budget.

This Gift-Giving Worksheet works as a reminder as you anticipate the total yearly cost for all upcom-

Gift-Giving Worksheet

	Name	Amount: Christmas	Birthday	(Month Due)	Other*
Parents					
Children					
Sisters/Brothers					
Friends					

* Other: Anniversaries, weddings, showers, new babies, Mother's Day, Father's Day, graduation, religious events.

ing events involving gifts. Remembering Christmas and birthdays generally is easy. Events such as Father's Day or your parents' anniversary, however, often are overlooked until the month they occur. Even if you don't buy gifts but send flowers or go out to dinner instead, include these costs in your plan. By outlining all the members of your family and your friends and all the events celebrated in your household on this worksheet, you have a handy total picture of what gift expenses to expect. You then can transfer these amounts to the "Gifts" section of the Yearly Budget Worksheet.

Gift-Giving Worksheet

	Name	Amount: Christmas	Birthday	(Month Due)	Other*
Grandparents					
Aunts/Uncles					
Nieces/Nephews					
Children's Friends					

* Other: Anniversaries, weddings, showers, new babies, Mother's Day, Father's Day, graduation, religious events.

Subscription Record

If you ever waited three months to receive your subscription or learned that your magazine gift took that long before it was ever received, you will appreciate having all this information at your fingertips.

Subscription Record

Publication:							
Subscription through: Agency Address							
Telephone							
Date Ordered							
Amount Paid							
Check # or Credit Card Used							
Length							
Expiration Date							
Arrival Date							
Gift For:							
Other							

Debt Payment Record

WHEN TO USE THIS WORKSHEET

If you are beginning to get deep in debt or just need a better idea of how much you still owe on all your bills such as medical expenses, car loan, finance company loan, credit cards, etc., this worksheet is an important part of your financial planning.

WHAT TO INCLUDE

The expenses to include are those you are unable to pay in full and must extend over a period of time (installment payments) such as automobile, home-equity, student or finance-company loans; medical, legal or family loans; IRS debt; and credit-card and airline-card charges. This worksheet will graphically show you how much you have paid, what you still owe and how much it is costing you to pay in installments. Remember, every penny you pay for interest is money you could have in your pocket if the bill were paid in full.

GETTING OUT OF DEBT

After paying off one debt, apply that same payment amount to another debt, preferably one with the highest interest, to shorten the term of that debt. As you continue to apply payments from paid-off debt to remaining debt, you will clearly see how soon and how much of your total debt will be paid off in one year's time.

By the following year, through the conscientious use of the worksheets in this workbook, you no longer may need this worksheet. Hurray!

As one reader put it, "This form makes the whole workbook worth hugging a thousand times!"

COST OF CREDIT PURCHASES

December Total Charges: $1,000
Annual Finance Rate: 18%

Total Interest Paid on $1,000

	Monthly Payment: $50	Monthly Payment: $25
Year 1	$ 144.00	$ 170.00
Year 2	54.00	144.00
Year 3		114.00
Year 4		77.00
Year 5		34.00
Year 6		0.77
Total Interest	$ 198.00	$ 540.00
Total Cost	$1,198.00	$1,540.00

Will you be paying off your $1,000 Christmas charges on one card from 1992 in 1998?

GETTING CONTROL OF YOUR FINANCES

When you reach the point where you use credit to your advantage, and only as a means of using someone else's money, and can pay the bill in full when it is due, you will know you truly have control of your finances!

MAKING MONEY INSTEAD OF SPENDING MONEY

Once you have gotten into the habit of making payments and applying extra money from paid-off debt to reducing the remaining debt, you will have acquired a great skill. When your debts are paid off, you can continue the payment schedule, only this time putting money into your savings and investments. All that money that was used to pay off the debt-plus-interest and penalty charges now can go toward your savings for you. Instead of spending money, you actually will be making money on the same payment amounts.

Best of all, you will feel encouraged, excited and confident!

Debt Payment Record

	Loans			Credit Cards		
CREDITOR						
Starting Date						
Total Balance Due						
Interest Rate						
January						
Amount Paid						
Interest/Penalty						
Balance Due						
February						
Amount Paid						
Interest/Penalty						
Balance Due						
March						
Amount Paid						
Interest/Penalty						
Balance Due						
April						
Amount Paid						
Interest/Penalty						
Balance Due						
May						
Amount Paid						
Interest/Penalty						
Balance Due						
June						
Amount Paid						
Interest/Penalty						
Balance Due						
July						
Amount Paid						
Interest/Penalty						
Balance Due						
August						
Amount Paid						
Interest/Penalty						
Balance Due						
September						
Amount Paid						
Interest/Penalty						
Balance Due						
October						
Amount Paid						
Interest/Penalty						
Balance Due						
November						
Amount Paid						
Interest/Penalty						
Balance Due						
December						
Amount Paid						
Interest/Penalty						
Balance Due						
Balance Due						

Debt Payment Record

						Total
Other (Medical, Legal, Personal, etc.)						

Credit-Card Purchase Record

To avoid a shocking bill at the end of the month, keep careful track of your credit-card charges. This way, you can anticipate what the bill will be and prepare for it by making the appropriate adjustments in your spending and your planning.

By knowing the status of your charges at all times you become much more selective and careful about impulse charging. When you reach this point, you know that you have learned how to keep from getting overextended and have taken one more step toward controlling your finances.

Credit-Card Purchase Record

Jan.		Feb.		Mar.		Apr.		May		June	
Billing Cycle Closing Date: ① _____		_____		_____		_____		_____		_____	
Purchases	Amount	Purchases	Amount	Purchases	Amount	Purchases	Amount	Purchases	Amount	Purchases	Amount
③ ³/Gas ②	14.91										
⁷/shoes	20.82										
Total											

HOW TO USE THIS CHART

First find out and enter the "Billing Cycle Closing Date." Then record all charges made during the month until that date so you know which purchases will be included on that month's upcoming bill. Purchases charged after that closing date should be entered in the next month's column (the month for which you actually will be billed). Jot down in the corner the date you made the charge. ③

① ②

Remember, this chart is flexible. If you use different cards frequently, then divide the monthly column into the necessary parts to keep the separate records. You also can carry an extra check register to record your charges for other cards. Make the chart work for you!

Credit-Card Purchase Record

July		Aug.		Sept.		Oct.		Nov.		Dec.	
Purchases	Amount	Purchases	Amount	Purchases	Amount	Purchases	Amount	Purchases	Amount	Purchases	Amount

Mail-Order Purchase Record

SHOPPING BY MAIL

Most mail or telephone purchases are through advertisements found in catalogs, brochures, newspapers and magazines, as well as on TV and radio. There are advantages to shopping by mail, including convenience and saving time. However, how many times have you ordered something by mail or telephone (trusting it would arrive in 30 to 60 days), and it never arrived? Chances are, you've had your share of mail-order frustrations and undelivered orders (which you may have even forgotten) and now recognize the value of keeping records for follow-up action.

HOW TO KEEP RECORDS

If orders do not arrive as scheduled and follow-up work is necessary, this Mail-Order Purchase Record will be a valuable time- and money-saver for you.

Use this chart for all items ordered even if they are free. Log necessary information related to any

Mail-Order Purchase Record

Date Ordered					
Item(s) Ordered Title, Description, Number, Quantity, Color					
Source (Magazine, TV, Catalog)					
Company Name Telephone Number Address					
Price					
Total Sent					
How Paid (Credit card, Check number, Money order, C.O.D.)					
Date Received					
Follow-Up Notes (Date called/wrote, Contact person, Action taken)					

purchases made by mail or telephone. When you happen to remember an item you ordered some time ago and realize it still has not arrived, you can go back to your records, see when you ordered the item, then follow up by telephone or mail, if necessary.

In some cases, it may be easier to cut out the advertisement with all the information given and tape it to the page, then fill in the "Total Sent" and "How Paid" sections. If you order a list of items from a catalog, make a copy of the order form and save it. On the chart, make a note of the order, the catalog date and how you paid for it.

When placing a telephone order, be especially careful to record all the information on the chart, including the name of the person who took your order.

FEDERAL TRADE COMMISSION (FTC) MAIL-ORDER RULE

The Mail-Order Rule of the Federal Trade Commission (FTC) requires companies to ship an order within the time period mentioned in their advertisements. If no time period is mentioned, the company is required to ship an order within 30 days of receipt of your payment. The company must notify you if it cannot make the shipment within 30 days and send you an option notice of either consenting to a delay or canceling the order for a refund.

For a free brochure on the Mail-Order Rule, write the Federal Trade Commission, Pennsylvania Avenue N.W. at 6th Street, Washington, DC 20580.

Mail-Order Purchase Record

Date Ordered					

Item(s) Ordered
  Title,
  Description,
  Number,
  Quantity,
  Color					

Source (Magazine, TV, Catalog)					

Company Name
  Telephone Number
  Address					

Price					
Total Sent					
How Paid (Credit card, Check number, Money order, C.O.D.)					
Date Received					
Follow-Up Notes (Date called/wrote, Contact person, Action taken)					

Monthly Expense Record

How many times have you asked yourself "Where did all my money go?" With these worksheets and with some firm self-discipline, you will easily know where all your money has gone as well as how much money has come in.

Begin by saving receipts and recording them daily or weekly before tossing them, or just keep a small notebook with you to record cash spent and transfer that information to this worksheet. With practice and determination, you will develop the habit of regularly recording all cash, checkbook and charged expenses.

Your payoff will be the sense of control you have over your finances and your finally being aware of your overall spending. Many people insist that they started saving much more money once they began recording all their expenses. They used to think that keeping detailed records in their check registers was enough. Eventually, they found that the check registers did not provide near so graphic and concise an answer to where the money was going as these worksheets.

Recording cash is important. Every time you write a check for cash or use the automated teller machine (ATM), write down where you actually spent that cash. Itemizing all the cash provides more valuable information for you than just recording "$50 cash" four times as an expense.

If you seem to have more month than money most of the time, remember your choices. You can reduce, postpone, modify or eliminate your spending. If you are not sure where to begin, a review of these filled-out worksheets will quickly show you which optional categories to begin with. Maybe you need to do more of your own home or car repairs, be more energy-conscious, eat out less, cut back on gifts or start car pooling or whatever fits your abilities and interests. When you do cut back, the results will be noticed immediately.

As you work with these worksheets, modify them to fit your unique life-style. The expense categories, net income, savings, investment and retirement sections are all provided as guidelines to set up your own system.

If you have tax-deductible expenses, note them here. If you want all your tax records kept together, you can use the handy Tax-Deductible Expense Record near the back of the book.

You will notice the emphasis on net income, not on gross income, throughout this workbook. The idea is to deal only with actual money and not record more information than you need to. The gross income information is usually on your check stubs. If you need to keep a record of your taxes, FICA and other deductions, you can use the "End-of-the-Year Tax Information" section on the bottom of the Summary-for-the-Year worksheet.

Monthly Expense Record

Net Income

SALARY/COMMISSIONS	Chris	Kim	TOTAL
	896.00		
		1,107.43	
	883.00		
		1,107.43	
		TOTAL INCOME	3,993.86
OTHER			
Yard Sale - 273			273.00
		TOTAL INCOME	4,266.86

Savings

(Describe)	
Reserve	745.00
(used other $257 this month)	
Emergency	215.00
TOTAL SAVINGS	960.00

Investments/Retirement

(See Payroll Deduction)	
TOTAL INVESTMENTS	

	Food			Household				Transportation			Personal		Medical	
	groceries	meals out school lunches	beverages	mainten. house yard pool	appliance furniture furnishings supplies	misc. postage copies bank chg. film	interest taxes	gas	auto mainten. wash license	transit tolls parking	clothing sewing cleaning	cosmetics hair massage	doctor dentist medicine vitamins	personal growth therapy
1	40.00	15.00						13.92						
2		7.50		20.34	33.67									
3	5.94							9.35				25.00		65.30
4			15.31						24.73		21.82		10.20	
5		28.98												
6														
7	44.48										15.03			
8													33.68	
9	67.10	7.50				29.00					43.98			
10								14.79						
11	7.25	14.22										19.00		
12													13.00	
13				14.76					6.95					
14														
15	10.53											21.46		
16		12.35						10.45			20.80			
17														
18	28.55	7.50												
19														
20	9.57										13.37			
21					23.00									65.30
22			11.08					15.65						
23				10.45										
24														
25	49.73													
26		7.50						9.35			15.41			
27						8.50								
28	19.52													
29				4.31										
30	67.10	27.34						19.95						
31	8.59													
Total	358.36	127.89	26.39	49.86	56.67	37.50	—	88.46	31.68	—	130.41	65.46	56.88	130.60

Monthly Expense Record

Fixed Expenses

Monthly	Amount	Monthly	Amount
Mortgage/Rent	784.00	Insurance:	
Gas/Fuel	73.00	House/Apt	
Electricity	89.00	Auto	
Water/Refuse		Life	54.00
Garbage/Sewer		Health (Payroll ded.)	
Telephone	53.21	Dental	
Cable	35.00	Disability	
Assoc. Fee			
Child Support			
Spousal Support			
TOTAL	1,034.21	TOTAL	54.00

Installment Expenses

Loans/Credit Cards	Amount
Visa	75.00
MC	50.00
Student Loan	50.00
Car Payment	211.00
TOTAL	386.00

Total Expenses

Total Fixed Expenses	1,088.21
Total Installment Expenses	386.00
Total Monthly Expenses from Below	1,704.75
GRAND TOTAL	3,178.96

+ Savings (960.00) = $4,138.96

	Recreation			Education		Children		General					
	vacation trips	entertain. video computer	sports hobbies lessons clubs	tuition supplies	books magazines software	childcare sitter	allowance toys school expense	pet vet supplies	gifts cards flowers	charitable contribut. church	work expense dues	prof. services lawyer CPA	other (explanation)
1							10.00			50.00			
2		3.21							40.00				
3													
4													
5							10.00						
6													
7										50.00			
8							3.57						
9			19.22										
10									3.59				
11					15.22								
12							10.00						
13										50.00			
14									10.56				
15							15.98						
16													
17		15.04											
18					23.78		10.00						
19									2.60	50.00			
20													
21													
22					39.00								
23							4.98						
24													
25										40.00			
26													
27							10.00						
28		57.84											
29													
30													
31													
Total	—	76.09	19.22	—	78.00	—	74.53	—	56.75	240.00	—	—	—

Monthly Expense Record

Net Income

SALARY/COMMISSIONS			TOTAL
	TOTAL INCOME		

OTHER		
TOTAL INCOME		

Savings

(Describe)	
TOTAL SAVINGS	

Investments/Retirement

TOTAL INVESTMENTS	

	Food		Household				Transportation			Personal		Medical	
	groceries	meals out school lunches	beverages	mainten. house yard pool	appliance furniture furnishings supplies	misc. postage copies bank chg. film	interest taxes	gas	auto mainten. wash license	transit tolls parking	clothing sewing cleaning	cosmetics hair massage	doctor dentist medicine vitamins	personal growth therapy
1														
2														
3														
4														
5														
6														
7														
8														
9														
10														
11														
12														
13														
14														
15														
16														
17														
18														
19														
20														
21														
22														
23														
24														
25														
26														
27														
28														
29														
30														
31														
Total														

Fixed Expenses

Monthly	Amount	Monthly	Amount
Mortgage/Rent		Insurance:	
Gas/Fuel		House/Apt	
Electricity		Auto	
Water/Refuse		Life	
Garbage/Sewer		Health	
Telephone		Dental	
Cable		Disability	
Assoc. Fee			
Child Support			
Spousal Support			
TOTAL		TOTAL	

Installment Expenses

Loans/Credit Cards	Amount
TOTAL	

Total Expenses

Total Fixed Expenses	
Total Installment Expenses	
Total Monthly Expenses from Below	
GRAND TOTAL	

	Recreation			Education		Children			General					
	vacation trips	entertain. video computer	sports hobbies lessons clubs	tuition supplies	books magazines software	childcare sitter	allowance toys school expense	pet vet supplies	gifts cards flowers	charitable contribut. church	work expense dues	prof. services lawyer CPA	other (explanation)	
1														
2														
3														
4														
5														
6														
7														
8														
9														
10														
11														
12														
13														
14														
15														
16														
17														
18														
19														
20														
21														
22														
23														
24														
25														
26														
27														
28														
29														
30														
31														
Total														

Monthly Expense Record

Net Income

			TOTAL
SALARY/COMMISSIONS			
		TOTAL INCOME	
OTHER			
		TOTAL INCOME	

Savings

(Describe)	
TOTAL SAVINGS	

Investments/Retirement

TOTAL INVESTMENTS	

	Food			Household				Transportation			Personal		Medical	
	groceries	meals out school lunches	beverages	mainten. house yard pool	appliance furniture furnishings supplies	misc. postage copies bank chg. film	interest taxes	gas	auto mainten. wash license	transit tolls parking	clothing sewing cleaning	cosmetics hair massage	doctor dentist medicine vitamins	personal growth therapy
1														
2														
3														
4														
5														
6														
7														
8														
9														
10														
11														
12														
13														
14														
15														
16														
17														
18														
19														
20														
21														
22														
23														
24														
25														
26														
27														
28														
29														
30														
31														
Total														

Monthly Expense Record

Fixed Expenses

Monthly	Amount	Monthly	Amount
Mortgage/Rent		Insurance:	
Gas/Fuel		House/Apt	
Electricity		Auto	
Water/Refuse		Life	
Garbage/Sewer		Health	
Telephone		Dental	
Cable		Disability	
Assoc. Fee			
Child Support			
Spousal Support			
TOTAL		TOTAL	

Installment Expenses

Loans/Credit Cards	Amount
TOTAL	

Total Expenses

Total Fixed Expenses	
Total Installment Expenses	
Total Monthly Expenses from Below	
GRAND TOTAL	

	Recreation			Education		Children		General					
	vacation trips	entertain. video computer	sports hobbies lessons clubs	tuition supplies	books magazines software	childcare sitter	allowance toys school expense	pet vet supplies	gifts cards flowers	charitable contribut. church	work expense dues	prof. services lawyer CPA	other (explanation)
1													
2													
3													
4													
5													
6													
7													
8													
9													
10													
11													
12													
13													
14													
15													
16													
17													
18													
19													
20													
21													
22													
23													
24													
25													
26													
27													
28													
29													
30													
31													
Total													

Monthly Expense Record

Balance Forward from Last Month:

Cash _____ Checking _____ Savings _____

Net Income

			TOTAL
SALARY/COMMISSIONS			
		TOTAL INCOME	
OTHER			
		TOTAL INCOME	

Savings

(Describe)	
TOTAL SAVINGS	

Investments/Retirement

TOTAL INVESTMENTS	

	Food			Household				Transportation			Personal		Medical	
	groceries	meals out school lunches	beverages	mainten. house yard pool	appliance furniture furnishings supplies	misc. postage copies bank chg. film	interest taxes	gas	auto mainten. wash license	transit tolls parking	clothing sewing cleaning	cosmetics hair massage	doctor dentist medicine vitamins	personal growth therapy
1														
2														
3														
4														
5														
6														
7														
8														
9														
10														
11														
12														
13														
14														
15														
16														
17														
18														
19														
20														
21														
22														
23														
24														
25														
26														
27														
28														
29														
30														
31														
Total														

Monthly Expense Record

Fixed Expenses

Monthly	Amount	Monthly	Amount
Mortgage/Rent		Insurance:	
Gas/Fuel		House/Apt	
Electricity		Auto	
Water/Refuse		Life	
Garbage/Sewer		Health	
Telephone		Dental	
Cable		Disability	
Assoc. Fee			
Child Support			
Spousal Support			
TOTAL		TOTAL	

Installment Expenses

Loans/Credit Cards	Amount
TOTAL	

Total Expenses

Total Fixed Expenses	
Total Installment Expenses	
Total Monthly Expenses from Below	
GRAND TOTAL	

	Recreation			Education		Children		General					
	vacation trips	entertain. video computer	sports hobbies lessons clubs	tuition supplies	books magazines software	childcare sitter	allowance toys school expense	pet vet supplies	gifts cards flowers	charitable contribut. church	work expense dues	prof. services lawyer CPA	other (explanation)
1													
2													
3													
4													
5													
6													
7													
8													
9													
10													
11													
12													
13													
14													
15													
16													
17													
18													
19													
20													
21													
22													
23													
24													
25													
26													
27													
28													
29													
30													
31													
Total													

Monthly Expense Record

Balance Forward from Last Month:

Cash _____ Checking _____ Savings _____

Net Income

			TOTAL
SALARY/COMMISSIONS			
		TOTAL INCOME	
OTHER			
		TOTAL INCOME	

Savings

(Describe)	
TOTAL SAVINGS	

Investments/Retirement

TOTAL INVESTMENTS	

	Food			Household				Transportation			Personal		Medical	
	groceries	meals out school lunches	beverages	mainten. house yard pool	appliance furniture furnishings supplies	misc. postage copies bank chg. film	interest taxes	gas	auto mainten. wash license	transit tolls parking	clothing sewing cleaning	cosmetics hair massage	doctor dentist medicine vitamins	personal growth therapy
1														
2														
3														
4														
5														
6														
7														
8														
9														
10														
11														
12														
13														
14														
15														
16														
17														
18														
19														
20														
21														
22														
23														
24														
25														
26														
27														
28														
29														
30														
31														
Total														

Monthly Expense Record APRIL

Fixed Expenses

Monthly	Amount	Monthly	Amount
Mortgage/Rent		Insurance:	
Gas/Fuel		House/Apt	
Electricity		Auto	
Water/Refuse		Life	
Garbage/Sewer		Health	
Telephone		Dental	
Cable		Disability	
Assoc. Fee			
Child Support			
Spousal Support			
TOTAL		TOTAL	

Installment Expenses

Loans/Credit Cards	Amount
TOTAL	

Total Expenses

Total Fixed Expenses	
Total Installment Expenses	
Total Monthly Expenses from Below	
GRAND TOTAL	

	Recreation			Education		Children		General					
	vacation trips	entertain. video computer	sports hobbies lessons clubs	tuition supplies	books magazines software	childcare sitter	allowance toys school expense	pet vet supplies	gifts cards flowers	charitable contribut. church	work expense dues	prof. services lawyer CPA	other (explanation)
1													
2													
3													
4													
5													
6													
7													
8													
9													
10													
11													
12													
13													
14													
15													
16													
17													
18													
19													
20													
21													
22													
23													
24													
25													
26													
27													
28													
29													
30													
31													
Total													

Monthly Expense Record

Net Income

			TOTAL
SALARY/COMMISSIONS			
		TOTAL INCOME	
OTHER			
		TOTAL INCOME	

Savings

(Describe)	
TOTAL SAVINGS	

Investments/Retirement

TOTAL INVESTMENTS	

	Food			Household					Transportation			Personal		Medical	
	groceries	meals out school lunches	beverages	mainten. house yard pool	appliance furniture furnishings supplies	misc. postage copies bank chg. film	interest taxes		gas	auto mainten. wash license	transit tolls parking	clothing sewing cleaning	cosmetics hair massage	doctor dentist medicine vitamins	personal growth therapy
1															
2															
3															
4															
5															
6															
7															
8															
9															
10															
11															
12															
13															
14															
15															
16															
17															
18															
19															
20															
21															
22															
23															
24															
25															
26															
27															
28															
29															
30															
31															
Total															

Monthly Expense Record

Fixed Expenses

Monthly	Amount	Monthly	Amount
Mortgage/Rent		Insurance:	
Gas/Fuel		House/Apt	
Electricity		Auto	
Water/Refuse		Life	
Garbage/Sewer		Health	
Telephone		Dental	
Cable		Disability	
Assoc. Fee			
Child Support			
Spousal Support			
TOTAL		TOTAL	

Installment Expenses

Loans/Credit Cards	Amount
TOTAL	

Total Expenses

Total Fixed Expenses	
Total Installment Expenses	
Total Monthly Expenses from Below	
GRAND TOTAL	

	Recreation			Education		Children		General						
	vacation trips	entertain. video computer	sports hobbies lessons clubs	tuition supplies	books magazines software	childcare sitter	allowance toys school expense	pet vet supplies	gifts cards flowers	charitable contribut. church	work expense dues	prof. services lawyer CPA	other (explanation)
1													
2													
3													
4													
5													
6													
7													
8													
9													
10													
11													
12													
13													
14													
15													
16													
17													
18													
19													
20													
21													
22													
23													
24													
25													
26													
27													
28													
29													
30													
31													
Total													

Monthly Expense Record

Net Income

SALARY/COMMISSIONS			TOTAL
		TOTAL INCOME	
OTHER			
		TOTAL INCOME	

Savings

(Describe)	
TOTAL SAVINGS	

Investments/Retirement

TOTAL INVESTMENTS	

	Food			Household				Transportation			Personal		Medical	
	groceries	meals out school lunches	beverages	mainten. house yard pool	appliance furniture furnishings supplies	misc. postage copies bank chg. film	interest taxes	gas	auto mainten. wash license	transit tolls parking	clothing sewing cleaning	cosmetics hair massage	doctor dentist medicine vitamins	personal growth therapy
1														
2														
3														
4														
5														
6														
7														
8														
9														
10														
11														
12														
13														
14														
15														
16														
17														
18														
19														
20														
21														
22														
23														
24														
25														
26														
27														
28														
29														
30														
31														
Total														

Monthly Expense Record

Fixed Expenses

Monthly	Amount	Monthly	Amount
Mortgage/Rent		Insurance:	
Gas/Fuel		House/Apt	
Electricity		Auto	
Water/Refuse		Life	
Garbage/Sewer		Health	
Telephone		Dental	
Cable		Disability	
Assoc. Fee			
Child Support			
Spousal Support			
TOTAL		TOTAL	

Installment Expenses

Loans/Credit Cards	Amount
TOTAL	

Total Expenses

Total Fixed Expenses	
Total Installment Expenses	
Total Monthly Expenses from Below	
GRAND TOTAL	

	Recreation			Education		Children		General					
	vacation trips	entertain. video computer	sports hobbies lessons clubs	tuition supplies	books magazines software	childcare sitter	allowance toys school expense	pet vet supplies	gifts cards flowers	charitable contribut. church	work expense dues	prof. services lawyer CPA	other (explanation)
1													
2													
3													
4													
5													
6													
7													
8													
9													
10													
11													
12													
13													
14													
15													
16													
17													
18													
19													
20													
21													
22													
23													
24													
25													
26													
27													
28													
29													
30													
31													
Total													

Monthly Expense Record

Balance Forward from Last Month:

Cash _____ Checking _____ Savings _____

Net Income

			TOTAL
SALARY/COMMISSIONS			
	TOTAL INCOME		
OTHER			
	TOTAL INCOME		

Savings

(Describe)	
TOTAL SAVINGS	

Investments/Retirement

TOTAL INVESTMENTS	

	Food			Household				Transportation			Personal		Medical	
	groceries	meals out school lunches	beverages	mainten. house yard pool	appliance furniture furnishings supplies	misc. postage copies bank chg. film	interest taxes	gas	auto mainten. wash license	transit tolls parking	clothing sewing cleaning	cosmetics hair massage	doctor dentist medicine vitamins	personal growth therapy
1														
2														
3														
4														
5														
6														
7														
8														
9														
10														
11														
12														
13														
14														
15														
16														
17														
18														
19														
20														
21														
22														
23														
24														
25														
26														
27														
28														
29														
30														
31														
Total														

Monthly Expense Record

Fixed Expenses

Monthly	Amount	Monthly	Amount
Mortgage/Rent		Insurance:	
Gas/Fuel		House/Apt	
Electricity		Auto	
Water/Refuse		Life	
Garbage/Sewer		Health	
Telephone		Dental	
Cable		Disability	
Assoc. Fee			
Child Support			
Spousal Support			
TOTAL		TOTAL	

Installment Expenses

Loans/Credit Cards	Amount
TOTAL	

Total Expenses

Total Fixed Expenses	
Total Installment Expenses	
Total Monthly Expenses from Below	
GRAND TOTAL	

	Recreation			Education		Children		General						
	vacation trips	entertain. video computer	sports hobbies lessons clubs	tuition supplies	books magazines software	childcare sitter	allowance toys school expense	pet vet supplies	gifts cards flowers	charitable contribut. church	work expense dues	prof. services lawyer CPA	other (explanation)	
1														
2														
3														
4														
5														
6														
7														
8														
9														
10														
11														
12														
13														
14														
15														
16														
17														
18														
19														
20														
21														
22														
23														
24														
25														
26														
27														
28														
29														
30														
31														
Total														

Monthly Expense Record

Net Income

		TOTAL	
SALARY/COMMISSIONS			
		TOTAL INCOME	
OTHER			
		TOTAL INCOME	

Savings

(Describe)	
TOTAL SAVINGS	

Investments/Retirement

TOTAL INVESTMENTS	

	Food			Household				Transportation			Personal		Medical	
	groceries	meals out school lunches	beverages	mainten. house yard pool	appliance furniture furnishings supplies	misc. postage copies bank chg. film	interest taxes	gas	auto mainten. wash license	transit tolls parking	clothing sewing cleaning	cosmetics hair massage	doctor dentist medicine vitamins	personal growth therapy
1														
2														
3														
4														
5														
6														
7														
8														
9														
10														
11														
12														
13														
14														
15														
16														
17														
18														
19														
20														
21														
22														
23														
24														
25														
26														
27														
28														
29														
30														
31														
Total														

Monthly Expense Record

Fixed Expenses

Monthly	Amount	Monthly	Amount
Mortgage/Rent		Insurance:	
Gas/Fuel		House/Apt	
Electricity		Auto	
Water/Refuse		Life	
Garbage/Sewer		Health	
Telephone		Dental	
Cable		Disability	
Assoc. Fee			
Child Support			
Spousal Support			
TOTAL		TOTAL	

Installment Expenses

Loans/Credit Cards	Amount
TOTAL	

Total Expenses

Total Fixed Expenses	
Total Installment Expenses	
Total Monthly Expenses from Below	
GRAND TOTAL	

	Recreation			Education		Children		General						
	vacation trips	entertain. video computer	sports hobbies lessons clubs	tuition supplies	books magazines software	childcare sitter	allowance toys school expense	pet vet supplies	gifts cards flowers	charitable contribut. church	work expense dues	prof. services lawyer CPA	other (explanation)	
1														
2														
3														
4														
5														
6														
7														
8														
9														
10														
11														
12														
13														
14														
15														
16														
17														
18														
19														
20														
21														
22														
23														
24														
25														
26														
27														
28														
29														
30														
31														
Total														

Monthly Expense Record

Balance Forward from Last Month:

Cash _____ Checking _____ Savings _____

Net Income

				TOTAL
SALARY/COMMISSIONS				
			TOTAL INCOME	
OTHER				
			TOTAL INCOME	

Savings

(Describe)	
TOTAL SAVINGS	

Investments/Retirement

TOTAL INVESTMENTS	

	Food		Household					Transportation			Personal		Medical	
	groceries	meals out school lunches	beverages	mainten. house yard pool	appliance furniture furnishings supplies	misc. postage copies bank chg. film	interest taxes	gas	auto mainten. wash license	transit tolls parking	clothing sewing cleaning	cosmetics hair massage	doctor dentist medicine vitamins	personal growth therapy
1														
2														
3														
4														
5														
6														
7														
8														
9														
10														
11														
12														
13														
14														
15														
16														
17														
18														
19														
20														
21														
22														
23														
24														
25														
26														
27														
28														
29														
30														
31														
Total														

Fixed Expenses

Monthly	Amount	Monthly	Amount
Mortgage/Rent		Insurance:	
Gas/Fuel		House/Apt	
Electricity		Auto	
Water/Refuse		Life	
Garbage/Sewer		Health	
Telephone		Dental	
Cable		Disability	
Assoc. Fee			
Child Support			
Spousal Support			
TOTAL		TOTAL	

Installment Expenses

Loans/Credit Cards	Amount
TOTAL	

Total Expenses

Total Fixed Expenses	
Total Installment Expenses	
Total Monthly Expenses from Below	
GRAND TOTAL	

	Recreation			Education		Children		General					
	vacation trips	entertain. video computer	sports hobbies lessons clubs	tuition supplies	books magazines software	childcare sitter	allowance toys school expense	pet vet supplies	gifts cards flowers	charitable contribut. church	work expense dues	prof. services lawyer CPA	other (explanation)
1													
2													
3													
4													
5													
6													
7													
8													
9													
10													
11													
12													
13													
14													
15													
16													
17													
18													
19													
20													
21													
22													
23													
24													
25													
26													
27													
28													
29													
30													
31													
Total													

Monthly Expense Record

Net Income

			TOTAL
SALARY/COMMISSIONS			
		TOTAL INCOME	
OTHER			
		TOTAL INCOME	

Savings

(Describe)	
TOTAL SAVINGS	

Investments/Retirement

TOTAL INVESTMENTS	

	Food			Household				Transportation			Personal		Medical	
	groceries	meals out school lunches	beverages	mainten. house yard pool	appliance furniture furnishings supplies	misc. postage copies bank chg. film	interest taxes	gas	auto mainten. wash license	transit tolls parking	clothing sewing cleaning	cosmetics hair massage	doctor dentist medicine vitamins	personal growth therapy
1														
2														
3														
4														
5														
6														
7														
8														
9														
10														
11														
12														
13														
14														
15														
16														
17														
18														
19														
20														
21														
22														
23														
24														
25														
26														
27														
28														
29														
30														
31														
Total														

Monthly Expense Record

Fixed Expenses

Monthly	Amount	Monthly	Amount
Mortgage/Rent		Insurance:	
Gas/Fuel		House/Apt	
Electricity		Auto	
Water/Refuse		Life	
Garbage/Sewer		Health	
Telephone		Dental	
Cable		Disability	
Assoc. Fee			
Child Support			
Spousal Support			
TOTAL		TOTAL	

Installment Expenses

Loans/Credit Cards	Amount
TOTAL	

Total Expenses

Total Fixed Expenses	
Total Installment Expenses	
Total Monthly Expenses from Below	
GRAND TOTAL	

	Recreation			Education		Children		General						
	vacation trips	entertain. video computer	sports hobbies lessons clubs	tuition supplies	books magazines software	childcare sitter	allowance toys school expense	pet vet supplies	gifts cards flowers	charitable contribut. church	work expense dues	prof. services lawyer CPA	other (explanation)	
1														
2														
3														
4														
5														
6														
7														
8														
9														
10														
11														
12														
13														
14														
15														
16														
17														
18														
19														
20														
21														
22														
23														
24														
25														
26														
27														
28														
29														
30														
31														
Total														

Monthly Expense Record

Balance Forward from Last Month:

Cash _____ Checking _____ Savings _____

Net Income

			TOTAL
SALARY/COMMISSIONS			
		TOTAL INCOME	
OTHER			
		TOTAL INCOME	

Savings

(Describe)	
TOTAL SAVINGS	

Investments/Retirement

TOTAL INVESTMENTS	

	Food			Household				Transportation			Personal		Medical	
	groceries	meals out school lunches	beverages	mainten. house yard pool	appliance furniture furnishings supplies	misc. postage copies bank chg. film	interest taxes	gas	auto mainten. wash license	transit tolls parking	clothing sewing cleaning	cosmetics hair massage	doctor dentist medicine vitamins	personal growth therapy
1														
2														
3														
4														
5														
6														
7														
8														
9														
10														
11														
12														
13														
14														
15														
16														
17														
18														
19														
20														
21														
22														
23														
24														
25														
26														
27														
28														
29														
30														
31														
Total														

Fixed Expenses

Monthly	Amount	Monthly	Amount
Mortgage/Rent		Insurance:	
Gas/Fuel		House/Apt	
Electricity		Auto	
Water/Refuse		Life	
Garbage/Sewer		Health	
Telephone		Dental	
Cable		Disability	
Assoc. Fee			
Child Support			
Spousal Support			
TOTAL		TOTAL	

Installment Expenses

Loans/Credit Cards	Amount
TOTAL	

Total Expenses

Total Fixed Expenses	
Total Installment Expenses	
Total Monthly Expenses from Below	
GRAND TOTAL	

	Recreation			Education		Children		General						
	vacation trips	entertain. video computer	sports hobbies lessons clubs	tuition supplies	books magazines software	childcare sitter	allowance toys school expense	pet vet supplies	gifts cards flowers	charitable contribut. church	work expense dues	prof. services lawyer CPA	other (explanation)	
1														
2														
3														
4														
5														
6														
7														
8														
9														
10														
11														
12														
13														
14														
15														
16														
17														
18														
19														
20														
21														
22														
23														
24														
25														
26														
27														
28														
29														
30														
31														
Total														

Monthly Expense Record

Balance Forward from Last Month:

Cash _____ Checking _____ Savings _____

Net Income

SALARY/COMMISSIONS			TOTAL
		TOTAL INCOME	
OTHER			
		TOTAL INCOME	

Savings

(Describe)	
TOTAL SAVINGS	

Investments/Retirement

TOTAL INVESTMENTS	

	Food			Household				Transportation			Personal		Medical	
	groceries	meals out school lunches	beverages	mainten. house yard pool	appliance furniture furnishings supplies	misc. postage copies bank chg. film	interest taxes	gas	auto mainten. wash license	transit tolls parking	clothing sewing cleaning	cosmetics hair massage	doctor dentist medicine vitamins	personal growth therapy
1														
2														
3														
4														
5														
6														
7														
8														
9														
10														
11														
12														
13														
14														
15														
16														
17														
18														
19														
20														
21														
22														
23														
24														
25														
26														
27														
28														
29														
30														
31														
Total														

Monthly Expense Record

Fixed Expenses

Monthly	Amount	Monthly	Amount
Mortgage/Rent		Insurance:	
Gas/Fuel		House/Apt	
Electricity		Auto	
Water/Refuse		Life	
Garbage/Sewer		Health	
Telephone		Dental	
Cable		Disability	
Assoc. Fee			
Child Support			
Spousal Support			
TOTAL		TOTAL	

Installment Expenses

Loans/Credit Cards	Amount
TOTAL	

Total Expenses

Total Fixed Expenses	
Total Installment Expenses	
Total Monthly Expenses from Below	
GRAND TOTAL	

	Recreation			Education		Children		General					
	vacation trips	entertain. video computer	sports hobbies lessons clubs	tuition supplies	books magazines software	childcare sitter	allowance toys school expense	pet vet supplies	gifts cards flowers	charitable contribut. church	work expense dues	prof. services lawyer CPA	other (explanation)
1													
2													
3													
4													
5													
6													
7													
8													
9													
10													
11													
12													
13													
14													
15													
16													
17													
18													
19													
20													
21													
22													
23													
24													
25													
26													
27													
28													
29													
30													
31													
Total													

Summary-for-the-Year Record/
End-of-the-Year Tax Information

The totals you have at the end of each month in the Monthly Expense Record Worksheet can be transferred to this section so you will have a total picture.

This Summary-for-the-Year Record is excellent for measuring your financial progress and setting your future goals.

Summary-for-the-Year Record

		JAN.	FEB.	MAR.	APR.	MAY	JUNE	JULY	AUG.	SEPT.	OCT.	NOV.	DEC.	Total	Mo. Avg.
Net Income	Salary/ Commission														
	Other														
Food	Groceries														
	School Lunches Meals Out														
	Beverages														
Household	Supplies, Maintenance, House, Yard, Pool														
	Appliance, Furniture, Furnishings, Supplies														
	Postage, Copies, Bank Charges, Miscellaneous, Film														
	Interest, Taxes														
Transportation	Gas														
	Automobile Maintenance, Wash, License														
	Transit, Tolls, Parking														
Personal	Clothing, Sewing, Cleaning														
	Cosmetics, Hair, Massage														
Medical	Doctor, Dentist, Medicine, Vitamins														
	Personal Growth Therapy														
Recreation	Vacation, Trips														
	Entertain., Video, Computer														
	Hobbies, Lessons, Sports, Clubs														

Summary for Monthly Savings/Investments/Retirement

	JAN.	FEB.	MAR.	APR.	MAY	JUNE	JULY	AUG.	SEPT.	OCT.	NOV.	DEC.	Total
Savings													
Investments													
Retirement													
Total													

		JAN.	FEB.	MAR.	APR.	MAY	JUNE	JULY	AUG.	SEPT.	OCT.	NOV.	DEC.	Total	Mo. Avg.
Education	Tuition, Supplies														
Education	Books, Magazines, Software														
Children	Child Care, Sitter														
Children	Allowance, Toys, School Expense														
General	Pet, Vet, Supplies														
General	Gifts, Cards, Flowers														
General	Charitable Contribut., Church														
General	Work Expense, Dues														
General	Prof. Serv., Lawyer, CPA														
General	Other														
Home	Mortgage, Rent, Asso. Fees														
Utilities	Gas, Electric, Water, Garbage, Phone, Cable														
Support	Child, Spousal														
Insurance	Home, Auto, Life, Health, Disability														
Installment															
Total	Monthly Expenses														

End-of-the-Year Tax Information

	JAN.	FEB.	MAR.	APR.	MAY	JUNE	JULY	AUG.	SEPT.	OCT.	NOV.	DEC.	Total
Federal													
State													
FICA													
Other Deductions													
Total													

Medical Expense Record

If you must keep additional records on medical expenses, use these worksheets. A space is provided for mileage, which at this writing is tax deductible. The column for "Insurance Reimbursements" is provided for those households paying the medical bills first before submitting claims or paying the differences not covered by insurance and wanting to keep this information separate. During tax time, this information will save you hours of preparation time.

Medical and Dental Expenses

Date	Mileage	To Whom Paid	Amount	Insurance Reimbursements
Total				
Total Amount Paid				
Total Reimbursed				
Total Medical Cost				

Medical Expense Record

Medical Expenses and Prescriptions				
Date	Mileage	To Whom Paid	Amount	Insurance Reimbursements
		Total		
		Total Amount Paid		
		Total Reimbursed		
		Total Medical Cost		

Tax-Deductible Expense Record

After you record your expenses on the Monthly Expense Record Worksheets, take a moment to jot down deductible expenses on the Tax-Deductible Expense Record so you have all your deductible expenses recorded in one place. When you prepare your next year's tax return, itemizing deductions will be an efficient process.

Each year, tax deductions may vary. This worksheet is designed to be a convenient record of all deductions applying to your circumstances and the current tax laws. Include categories such as education, professional or union dues, child care, alimony, casualty losses, etc. If you have regular or multiple deductions in one category, the Multiple Tax-Deductible Expenses Record may be more convenient for recording those records.

Tax-Deductible Expense Record

Date	Description (Donation/Payment To)	Check Number	Amount/Value: Taxes/ Interest	Charitable Contribution		
		Total				

Multiple Tax-Deductible Expenses Record

Category: _____

Date	Description	Amount
	Total	

Category: _____

Date	Description	Amount
	Total	

Miscellaneous Expense Record

A variety of additional generic worksheets are provided for other records, such as major household purchases, car expenses, college costs, etc. Use any of these or the other variety of worksheets in this workbook to best fit your particular needs.

Record of_____   **Miscellaneous Expense Record Year 19____**

	JAN.	FEB.	MAR.	APR.	MAY	JUNE	JULY	AUG.	SEPT.	OCT.	NOV.	DEC.	TOTAL
Total													

Miscellaneous Expense Record

Date	To Whom Paid/Service	Amount
	Total	

Date	To Whom Paid/Service	Amount
	Total	

Investment/Savings Record

YOUR INVESTMENT PICTURE

If you followed the suggestions and guidelines in this workbook, you probably already have or soon will have some basic savings and investments.

Whether you have money in company savings plans, inherited some stocks and bonds, invested in mutual funds, changed your savings from passbooks to certificates of deposit (CDs) or money markets or opened an Individual Retirement Account (IRA), it is important to keep all your records in one place and know what you have. These records are extremely useful for preparing income tax, completing financial statements and helping your heirs in the event of an unexpected death.

As with personal finances, if you don't pay attention to your investments or keep careful records of them, you may easily forget them. Soon it may be hard to remember just exactly where you put those IRAs that you purchased sometime in 1988 and 1991. What rates are they getting? What are the maturity dates?

Or maybe through your parents or a divorce, you acquired some stocks that are just "sitting" in an account and you really don't know what you have. With today's fast-paced life-style, it is easy to leave the responsibility of knowing what you own to someone else—a banker, a broker or an accountant, but by doing so, you sacrifice an understanding and awareness of your total financial picture.

The Investment/Savings Record worksheet provides a place for recording key information about your various investments. The space on the right allows for a periodic follow-up of your current yield. The headings are used as a guideline. If necessary,

change them to make them appropriate for your investments.

If you anticipate frequent changes, you should record general information at the beginning of the year here and use the other worksheets in this section of the workbook to record your year's investment and savings activity. You can modify the Savings Activity Record, Retirement Savings Record or Miscellaneous Expense Record to fit your needs. The important point is to be sure that you have recorded all the information for each of your investments and have it all in one convenient place.

RESERVE FUNDS

Use this section of the Investment/Saving Record to record information about your liquid-asset accounts (money you have available for immediate use without withdrawal penalties). These include investments in money markets or savings in your bank and/or credit union.

If you have ongoing monthly savings activity, you can use the Savings Activity Record worksheet to record your month-to-month transactions. On that page, you can list your savings for upcoming taxes or insurance (reserve account), unexpected car or home repairs (emergency account) or vacation and Christmas savings (goal account).

RETIREMENT

Record your retirement savings programs information here. Your monthly savings activity can be recorded on the Retirement Savings Record in this section. These programs range from savings funded and/or established by your employer, to personal IRAs, Keoghs, company pensions and other tax-sheltered investments.

A wide variety of employee-retirement programs are offered through schools, hospitals, government and private firms. It is easy to forget or ignore these funds for they often are only shown as paycheck deductions. Pay attention to and gather up the necessary information as outlined in this section so you are familiar with your current and past retirement programs.

SHORT- AND LONG-TERM HOLDINGS

Record your investments held for short or extended periods in the Investment/Savings Record. Some of these investments, such as CDs, T-bills, bonds, etc., will have fixed rates or time periods and this information should be noted on the worksheet. Other securities (stocks, mutual funds, options) may change yields, time frames and prices daily. Because this worksheet has limited space for all the variable information, use this worksheet for beginning- and end-of-the-year summaries.

If you frequently buy, sell and actively get involved with your investments, you already may have an investment portfolio with all the necessary information. On the other hand, if you do not do much

with your investments, especially securities, *the information on this worksheet will be extremely helpful for tax, loan or net-worth purposes.*

OTHER INVESTMENTS

Your investments, such as real estate (other than personal residence), collectibles, trusts, limited or general partnerships, etc., also would be recorded here. If the majority of those other investments are quite extensive, however, you probably have them recorded through another system. If so, indicate where you have those records and those of any of your other investments listed on this worksheet.

MAINTAINING CONTROL OF YOUR FINANCES

As you gather your investment information, you may find you need to develop your own follow-up system for those long-range investments with maturity dates. Start a file and keep a copy of these worksheets for each year. Highlight the maturity dates so you have a quick reference.

These worksheets, along with the others you have used in this workbook, will help you to record all your financial information in one place, thus staying organized and aware of your finances!

Investment/Savings Record

Reserve Funds

Name of Institution	Type	Account Number	Date Opened	Amount Invested	Interest Rate	Owned by (husband, wife, joint)

Retirement Accounts

Where Held	Type and Name	Account Number	Purchase Date	Amount Invested	Interest Rate	Maturity Date

Short- and Long-Term Holdings

Where Held	Type and Name	Certificate/ Account Number	Purchase Date	Amount Invested	Number of Shares	Unit Price	Dividend/ Interest Rate

Other

Location/Name	Date Purchased	Cost	Monthly/Yearly Income	Location of Records

Investment/Savings Record

Reserve Funds

Contact Name/Telephone	Location of Records	Follow-Up Information (date, balance, current yield)

Retirement Accounts

Owned by (husband, wife, joint)	Contact Name/Telephone	Location of Records	Date Sold	Net Proceeds	Gain/ Loss	Additional Notes (roll-over information)

Short- and Long-Term Holdings

Date/Amount Dividend Paid	Maturity Date	Owned By (husband, wife, joint)	Contact Name/Telephone	Location of Records	Date Sold	Number of Shares Sold	Net Proceeds	Gain/ Loss

Other

Additional Notes (date sold, total proceeds, etc.)

Savings Activity Record

Emergency

Institution: _____   Account Number: _____

	JAN.	FEB.	MAR.	APR.	MAY	JUNE	JULY	AUG.	SEPT.	OCT.	NOV.	DEC.
Deposits												
Withdrawals												
Interest earned												
Balance												

Reserve

Institution: _____   Account Number: _____

	JAN.	FEB.	MAR.	APR.	MAY	JUNE	JULY	AUG.	SEPT.	OCT.	NOV.	DEC.
Deposits												
Withdrawals												
Interest earned												
Balance												

Goals/Christmas

Institution: _____   Account Number: _____

	JAN.	FEB.	MAR.	APR.	MAY	JUNE	JULY	AUG.	SEPT.	OCT.	NOV.	DEC.
Deposits												
Withdrawals												
Interest earned												
Balance												

Other

Institution: _____   Account Number: _____

	JAN.	FEB.	MAR.	APR.	MAY	JUNE	JULY	AUG.	SEPT.	OCT.	NOV.	DEC.
Deposits												
Withdrawals												
Interest earned												
Balance												

Retirement Savings Record

Name

Date	Program (IRA, 401(k), etc.): _____ _____ _____			Date	Program (IRA, 401(k), etc.): _____ _____ _____		
Total				**Total**			

Name

Date	Program (IRA, 401(k), etc.): _____ _____ _____			Date	Program (IRA, 401(k), etc.): _____ _____ _____		
Total				**Total**			

Net-Worth Statement

An important step in gaining financial control is to take an accounting of what your total financial worth is. Every year, your net worth should be tabulated to enable you to review your progress and compare it with your financial goals. In addition, a Net-Worth Statement is a valuable aid in planning your estate and establishing a record for loan and insurance purposes.

Net-Worth Statement

Assets—What You Own	
Cash: On Hand	_____
Checking Account	_____
Savings Accounts	_____
Money Markets	_____
Other	_____
Cash Value Life Insurance	_____
Real Estate/Property:	
Home	_____
Land	_____
Other	_____
Investments: (Market Value)	
Certificates of Deposit	_____
Stocks	_____
Bonds	_____
Mutual Funds	_____
Annuities	_____
IRAs	_____
401(k) or 403(b) Plans	_____
Pension Plan	_____
Other	_____
Loans Receivable	_____
Personal Property: (Present Value)	
Automobiles	_____
Recreational Vehicle/Boat	_____
Home Furnishings	_____
Appliances and Furniture	_____
Collections	_____
Jewelry and Furs	_____
Other	_____
	_____
	_____
Total Assets	

Liabilities—What You Owe	
Current Debts:	
Household	_____
Medical	_____
Credit Cards	_____
Department Store Cards	_____
Back Taxes	_____
Legal	_____
Other	_____
	_____
Mortgages:	
Home	_____
Land	_____
Other	_____
Loans:	
Bank/Finance Company	_____
Bank/Finance Company	_____
Automobiles	_____
Recreational Vehicle/Boat	_____
Education	_____
Life Insurance	_____
Personal (from family or friends)	_____
Other	_____
	_____
	_____
	_____
Total Liabilities	

Total Assets minus Total Liabilities = **Net Worth** _____

Child-Support Records

KEEPING RECORDS

After a divorce, it is so easy for depression, anger, fear and loneliness to interfere with practical thoughts and actions.

During this time, credit problems often crop up. This is not because you are incapable of managing your money, but often because you suddenly are overwhelmed with handling all the aspects of family life and household maintenance. Due dates, bills and paperwork may just seem to get away from you.

Keeping proper records of child-support payments, children's expenses and pertinent custody information is extremely important. However, because of the demands of trying to meet the physical and emotional needs of your children and yourself, these records often are neglected or are never established.

The following worksheets were designed to help remove some of the burden of keeping important records. The worksheets provide guidelines to help you remember what records you should keep and provide you with a tool for having all your necessary information and records in one place. By organizing and controlling this aspect of your life, you will be better equipped to move on to other pressing issues that you face every day.

If you are the noncustodial parent making the child-support payments, recording the information called for can be just as important for you. If you must prove what amount and when a support payment actually was made, received and cashed, or must prove other significant information for tax or legal purposes, you will have the necessary records.

Utilize and modify the worksheets in this book so that you can record information that is unique to your needs. For example, you may want to use the Medical and Dental Expense section of this workbook for keeping detailed records of who paid a medical expense, the insurance deductible or the difference not paid by insurance.

When using these worksheets, be aware that the state and federal laws and regulations vary. *The worksheets and text are not a substitute for legal advice from your local attorney. Consult with your attorney for any questions in this section.*

CHILD-SUPPORT PAYMENT RECORD

These records are critical when you need help from your local enforcement agency because of late, short or missing payments. The "Amount Due" column is for the monthly child-support payment as ① ordered. Enter the amount received under *the month* it was due. If no payment was received that month, note that under "Amount Received." Because these ② payments may vary from once a week, or once a month, to sporadically for the year, you will have to modify this column to fit your needs.

Record the other related child-support obligations as ordered by the divorce decree, such as ③ medical insurance premium, unreimbursed medical expense, tuition, dues, etc. Keep a copy of your decree, stating the terms, payment, custody, visitation and conditions of support in a convenient file.

Note under "Additional Information" if an item was substituted in lieu of a child-support payment. ④ Be sure to check with your attorney if this is an *acceptable form of child support.* If you do not wish to accept an item in lieu of a payment, ask your attorney if written notice should be given. If so, be sure to keep a copy.

When recording the institution, number and date ⑤ of the check or money order, use the symbols shown to indicate how the payment was made. If possible, keep a copy of all checks, money orders and envelopes. These copies will be helpful if a court or social agency ever needs to review your records in the event that there is an excessive lag between the date of the check and the date it was sent, or payment was stopped on a check or money order you received. Be sure to note if you are unable to make a copy of the checks, money orders or envelopes.

You will find that this worksheet will contain some of your most important records. Stay with it.

THE COST OF RAISING CHILDREN

If you need or want to analyze the cost of raising your children, to show the use of support provided or to demonstrate the need for increased support, use the Monthly Expense Record section.

Enter all your children's daily expenses along with all your other expenses on the Monthly Expense Record pages. Modify the headings to fit your individual needs. Use a highlighter, colored pencil or check mark to show which expenses are the children's. Total the children's expenses in the columns that apply and record the total at the bottom of the page below the family total. If you have a question about allocating expenses shared by you and your children, ask your local attorney.

Another method used by some families for keeping accurate records is a separate checking account and/or a credit card used strictly for children's expenses. Use the method that works best for you.

If you save all your receipts in envelopes labeled for the different categories, you can file these in your filing system.

CHILD-SUPPORT ENFORCEMENT AND CHILD-VISITATION RECORDS

In 1984, Congress passed the "Child-Support Enforcement Amendments of 1984" that strengthens the child-support enforcement laws throughout the country. The information you record will be invaluable if you ever need the services of a Child-Support Enforcement Bureau in your state to help you collect past-due child support.

If you would like more information about Child-Support Enforcement, write the Consumer Information Center, Dept. 628 M, Pueblo, CO 81009, and ask for a free copy of "Kids, They're Worth Every Penny: Handbook on Child-Support Enforcement," provided by the Office of Child Support Enforcement in Washington, D.C.

REDUCED ANXIETY

These worksheets cannot take away the pain. They can, however, help reduce some of the anxiety associated with the aftermath of a divorce. As you start taking charge of your situation and gain new knowledge, you will regain self-confidence and self-esteem in the process.

Best of luck to you!

Child-Support Payment Record

Balance Due (from previous year) $_____

Month	① Amount Due	② Amount Received	Amount Past Due	⑤ Number on: x—$ Order ✓—Check $—Cash	Date on: x—$ Order ✓—Check $—Cash	Date Payment Received	⑤ Institution and Account Number	③ Other Expenses*	④ Additonal Information/ Action Taken (check status, gifts, etc.)
JAN.									
FEB.									
MAR.									
APR.									
MAY									
JUNE									
JULY									
AUG.									
SEPT.									
OCT.									
NOV.									
DEC.									
Total									

* Stipulated by decree

Child-Support Enforcement Record

Noncustodial Parent		Child-Support Enforcement Office

Noncustodial Parent

Full Name

_____

Last-Known Address(es)

_____

_____

_____

Address Dates _____

Home Telephone

_____

Social Security Number

_____

Birth Date/Place _____

_____

Height _____ Weight _____

Occupation

_____

Last-Known Employer(s)

_____

_____

Address

_____

_____

_____

_____

Address Dates _____

Work Telephone

_____

_____

Child-Support Enforcement Office

Address

_____

_____

_____

Telephone Number

_____

Case Worker's Name/Telephone

_____

_____

Case Number

_____

Court Order Number

_____

Note: Get a Birth Registration Card from your Vital Statistics Office. This will have all your children's information printed on it so you will have the information handy.

Child-Visitation Record

Dates of Visitation											
JAN.	FEB.	MAR.	APR.	MAY	JUNE	JULY	AUG.	SEPT.	OCT.	NOV.	DEC.

Recommended Reading

The following books are recommended because of their total focus or special sections on budgeting, credit, debt, spending, money attitudes and recovery issues. If managing money is new for you, these books offer a variety of ideas, approaches and information to help you get started. These books can provide complementary information as you do the practical hands-on work with *The Budget Kit: The Common Cent$ Money Management Workbook.*

Conquer Your Debt: How To Solve Your Credit Problems, by William K. Brunette (Prentice Hall, 1990).

Consumer Reports Money Saving Tips for Good Times and Bad, by Walter B. Leonard and the editors of Consumer Reports Books (Consumer Reports Books, 1992).

Clearing Your Credit: How To Repair Your Credit Without an MBA, a CPA, or a BMW, by Charlene B. Brown (United Resource Books, 1988).

Creating Money: Keys to Abundance, by Sanaya Roman and Duane Packer (H. J. Kramer Inc., 1988).

Credit, Cash and Co-Dependency: The Money Connection, by Yvonne Kaye, PhD (Health Communications Inc., 1991).

Cure Your Money Ills: Improve Your Self-Esteem Through Personal Budgeting, by Michael R. Slavit (R&E Publishers, 1992).

Cut Your Bills in Half: Thousands of Tips To Save Thousands of Dollars, by the editors of Rodale Press (Rodale Press, 1989).

Financial Fitness for Newlyweds: A Complete, Quick and Easy-To-Use Guide to Financial Security—Designed Especially for Couples, by Elizabeth S. Lewin, CFP (Facts on File Publications, 1984).

Financial Self-Defense, by Charles Givens (Simon & Schuster, 1990).

Fresh Start!: Surviving Money Troubles, Rebuilding Your Credit, Recovering Before and After Bankruptcy, by John Ventura (Dearborn Financial Publishing, Inc., 1992).

Get Rich Slow, by Tama McAleese (Career Press, 1990).

How To Be a Financially Secure Woman: An Expert's Guide for the Woman Who Wants a Life of Financial Independence, by Mary Elizabeth Schlayer, EdD (Ballantine Books, 1987).

How To Get Out of Debt, Stay Out of Debt and Live Prosperously, by Jerrold Mundis (Bantam Books, 1988). Based on the proven principles and techniques of Debtors Anonymous.

How To Stop Fighting about Money and Make Some, by Adriane G. Berg (Newmarket Press, 1988).

How To Survive Without a Salary: Learning How To Live the Conserver Lifestyle, by Charles Long (Warwich Publishing Group, 1991).

How To Turn Your Money Life Around: The Money Books for Women, by Ruth Hayden (Health Communications Inc., 1992).

Kiplinger's Make Your Money Grow, by Theodore J. Miller, editor of Changing Times magazine (Kiplinger Books, 1988).

Making the Most of Your Money: Smart Ways To Create Wealth and Plan Your Finances in the 90's, by Jane Bryant Quinn (Simon & Schuster, 1991).

Me and My Money; Book One: Writing a Money Autobiography, by Karen McCall (Financial Recovery Press, 1990).

Money, How To Get It, Keep It, and Make It Grow, by Tama McAleese (Career Press, 1991).

Money for Life: The "Money Makeover" That Will End Your Worries and Secure Your Dreams, by Steve Crowley (Simon & Schuster, 1991).

Money Grows on Trees: How To Make, Manage and Master Money, by Alton Howard (Howard Publishers, 1991).

Money Love: How To Get the Money You Deserve for Whatever You Want, by Jerry Gilles (Warner Books, 1988).

1001 Ways To Cut Your Expenses, by Jonathan D. Pond (Dell Publishing, 1992).

Our Money Ourselves: Money Management for Each Stage of a Woman's Life, by Ginita Wall, CPA, CFP, and the editors of Consumer Reports Books (Consumer Reports Books, 1992).

Pearl Polto's Easy Guide to Good Credit, by Pearl B. Polto and Bob Oskam (Berkley Books, 1990).

Penny Pinching: How To Lower Your Everyday Expenses Without Lowering Your Standard of Living, by Lee and Barbara Simmons (Bantam Books, 1991).

Prospering Woman: A Complete Guide To Achieving the Full Abundant Life, by Ruth Ross, PhD (Bantam Books, 1985).

Safe Money in Tough Times: A Step by Step Action Plan To Protect You and Your Family in 1991, by Jonathan Pond (Dell Publishing, 1991).

Shopaholics: Serious Help for Addicted Spenders, by Janet E. Damon (Price Stern Sloan, 1988).

Terry Savage Talks Money: The Common-Sense Guide to Money Matters, by Terry Savage (Dearborn Financial Publishing, Inc., 1990).

The New Money Workbook for Women: A Step by Step Guide To Managing Your Personal Finances, by Carole Phillips (Brick House Publishing Co., 1988).

The New York Times Book of Personal Finance, by Leonard Sloane (Times Books, 1992).

Turn Chaos into Cash: The Complete Guide To Organizing and Managing Your Personal Finances, by Jean Ross Peterson (Betterway Publications, Inc., 1989).

Wealth Without Risk, by Charles Givens (Simon & Schuster, 1988).

Women and Money: A Guide for the 90s, by Anita Jones-Lee (Barron's, 1991).

Your Wealth-Building Years, by Adriane G. Berg (Newmarket Press, 1991).

RECOMMENDED READING

Index

Notes

Notes

Notes

Notes

Notes